GOOD HOUSEKEEPING
Complete Book of
Cake Decorating

GOOD HOUSEKEEPING
Complete Book of
Cake Decorating

by Good Housekeeping Institute

illustrated by Glenn Steward and Marilyn Day

published in collaboration with
Tate & Lyle Refineries Limited

EBURY PRESS *London*

Published by Ebury Press
National Magazine House
72 Broadwick Street
London W1V 2BP

First impression 1978
Second impression 1979
Third impression 1980
Fourth impression 1981
Fifth impression 1982
Sixth impression 1983
Seventh impression 1983
Eighth impression 1984

ISBN 0 85223 129 6

Editor Barbara Argles
Home economist Janet Marsh
Designer Derek Morrison
Colour photography by Bryce Attwell

Jacket photograph shows
Front Apricot ribbon cake (page 82), Lily-of-the-valley
wedding cake (page 72), Marzipan flower cakes (page 62)
Back Winter gingerbread house (page 106),
Feather-iced cakes (page 63)

Filmset by Advanced Filmsetters (Glasgow) Ltd
Printed and bound by
New Interlitho s.p.a., Milan

Contents

Handy cookery charts

CONVERSION TO METRIC MEASUREMENTS

The metric measures in the icing and cake recipes in this book are based on a 25 g unit instead of the ounce (28.35 g). Slight adjustments to this basic conversion standard were necessary in some recipes to achieve satisfactory results.

If you want to convert your own recipes from imperial to metric, we suggest you use the same 25 g unit, and use 600 ml in place of 1 pint, with the British Standard 5-ml and 15-ml spoons replacing the old variable teaspoons and table-spoons. These adaptations will sometimes give a slightly smaller recipe quantity and may require a shorter cooking time.

Note Sets of British Standard metric measuring spoons are available in the following sizes — 2.5 ml, 5 ml, 10 ml and 15 ml.

For more general reference, the following tables will be helpful.

METRIC CONVERSION SCALE

| | **Liquid** | | | **Solid** | |
Imperial	Exact conversion	Recommended ml	Imperial	Exact conversion	Recommended g
$\frac{1}{4}$ pint	142 ml	150 ml	1 oz	28.35 g	25 g
$\frac{1}{2}$ pint	284 ml	300 ml	2 oz	56.7 g	50 g
1 pint	568 ml	600 ml	4 oz	113.4 g	100 g
$1\frac{1}{2}$ pints	851 ml	900 ml	8 oz	226.8 g	225 g
$1\frac{3}{4}$ pints	992 ml	1 litre	12 oz	340.2 g	350 g
			14 oz	397.0 g	400 g
			16 oz (1 lb)	453.6 g	450 g

For quantities of $1\frac{3}{4}$ pints and over, litres and fractions of a litre have been used.

1 kilogram (kg) equals 2.2 lb.

Note Follow either the metric or the imperial measures in the recipes as they are not interchangeable.

OVEN TEMPERATURE CHART

°C	°F	Gas mark
110	225	$\frac{1}{4}$
130	250	$\frac{1}{2}$
140	275	1
150	300	2
170	325	3
180	350	4
190	375	5
200	400	6
220	425	7
230	450	8
240	475	9

CENTIMETRES – INCHES

0.5 cm	$\frac{1}{4}$ in	10 cm	4 in	30.5 cm	12 in
1 cm	$\frac{1}{2}$ in	12.5 cm	5 in	38 cm	15 in
2.5 cm	1 in	15 cm	6 in	45.5 cm	18 in
4 cm	$1\frac{1}{2}$ in	18 cm	7 in	51 cm	20 in
5 cm	2 in	20.5 cm	8 in		
6.5 cm	$2\frac{1}{2}$ in	23 cm	9 in		
7.5 cm	3 in	25.5 cm	10 in		

See also the chart on page 71 giving the quantities of almond paste and royal icing needed for square or round cakes, and the chart on page 119 for rich fruit cake ingredient quantities for any sized square or round cake.

Foreword

This is a practical guide to the fascinating and enjoyable art of cake decorating. For what can give more delight to your family and friends than a cake that looks as good as it tastes?

Here you will find design ideas, created in the Good Housekeeping Institute, for all occasions from the simplest tea party to a golden wedding celebration. The list includes sponge and sandwich cakes, small cakes, wedding, birthday, anniversary and Christmas cakes. There is a special section on children's party cakes with fun ideas for a ginger-bread house, a castle, a butterfly and many more. All the designs have detailed step-by-step line drawings with captions, as well as an illustration of the finished cake. Follow these and it's easy.

Icing technique is a skill that needs to be acquired, like any other. If you are a beginner, read Chapter 1 carefully for advice on types of equipment and icings. Spend a little time trying out the various designs and patterns so that when next you want to serve a decorated cake, you will set to with complete confidence. Chapter 2 gives lots of ideas for making your own cake decorations. Recipes for the icings and for the cakes themselves are provided as well.

There is a great sense of achievement to be had from producing beautifully decorated cakes, whether simple or more advanced, in your own home. The *Good Housekeeping Complete Book of Cake Decorating* shows you how to turn out professional results every time.

Good Housekeeping Institute

All you need to know about icing

Equipment

As cake icing becomes a more popular hobby the range of cake icing equipment available increases. It can be very confusing for the beginner to know which is essential equipment and which is a gadget that will stay in the kitchen drawer unused. You can in fact start with as little as one or two icing nozzles, plenty of greaseproof paper to make icing bags and everyday kitchen equipment. As long as the basic techniques are mastered, the results will be good. As you become more interested in the subject and more familiar with the techniques you will know which other equipment you need.

One general rule to follow when buying equipment is to purchase the best you can afford. Except for icing bags, it is unlikely you will need to buy items more than once and good quality icing equipment should last a life time.

Nozzles, pipes or tubes

Throughout the book, only the eight nozzles pictured right have been used, to achieve all the designs illustrated.

There are a number of makes available but when buying any nozzle look for one as perfect as possible. The seam running down the side of the nozzle should be well joined and not misshapen. The cut-outs at the tip of the nozzle should be precise, especially at the side join. Check that plain writing nozzles are perfectly round at the tip and that rosette pipes are cut evenly.

The style of the nozzle will vary — select one with a straight side and without a screw collar if it is to be used in a greaseproof paper or nylon icing bag. The nozzle with an attached screw collar is designed to be used with the older style icing pump or bags with special fitments. Larger nozzles designed mainly for piping creamed potato, meringue and fresh cream can also be used for piping icing on larger designs.

To clean

To clean icing nozzles, carefully push out any surplus icing with a finger and leave to soak overnight in a bowl of warm water. Dry thoroughly before storing.

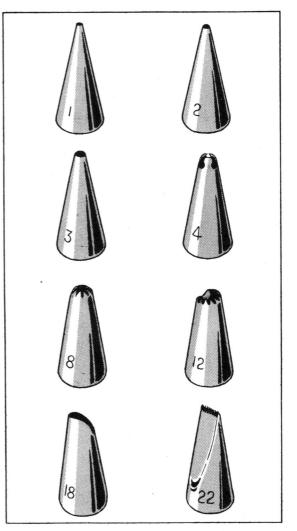

The eight nozzles used throughout the book
No. 1   Fine plain (writing) nozzle
No. 2   Medium plain (writing) nozzle
No. 3   Thicker plain (writing) nozzle
No. 4   Three point star (trefoil) nozzle
No. 8   Eight point star nozzle
No. 12   Shell nozzle
No. 18   Petal nozzle
No. 22   Basket (ribbon) nozzle

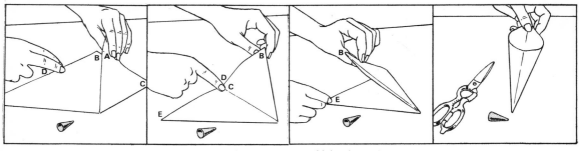

Folding a greaseproof icing bag

Greaseproof icing bags

The simplest icing bag to use with the nozzles is the hand-made greaseproof icing bag, simply folded from a square piece of good quality greaseproof paper.

1 Fold a 25·5-cm (10-in) square of grease-proof paper in half to form a triangle.

2 Fold point A to point B on a flat surface and crease the greaseproof paper.

3 Fold point C to point D, and crease the greaseproof paper.

4 Fold point B to point E, and crease the greaseproof paper.

5 Lift the folded greaseproof bag from the surface and hold in one hand where points A, B and E meet. Carefully shape into a cone with the other hand.

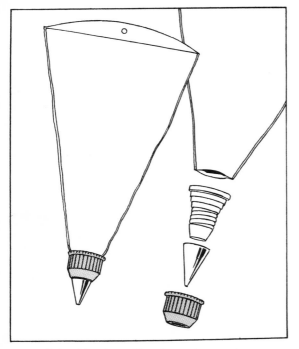

Nylon icing bag with collar and connector

6 Staple or fold the three points of paper over twice and crease well to secure tightly.

7 Cut off the tip of the cone with a pair of scissors and insert the nozzle; cutting just the tip of the greaseproof icing bag away for plain or writing nozzles and a little more for shaped nozzles.

The greaseproof icing bag is ideal when piping small quantities of butter, glacé or royal icing. It can be opened and refilled successfully but care must be taken to ensure that the bag does not split or come unfolded. Never overfill.

Nylon icing bags

For larger quantities of icing or general ease of handling, the nylon bag is much better. They are available in a range of sizes; choose one not too large as it is easier to handle small quantities and refill the bag when necessary. To use with icing nozzles you need a collar and connector. The polythene connector is inserted into the bag, the nozzle is placed inside the collar and is then screwed on to the connector. The great advantage of this type of bag is that different nozzles can be interchanged without requiring a fresh bag of icing.

The advantage of using greaseproof or nylon icing bags is that the icing inside reacts immediately to the pressure applied, thus enabling easy control during icing.

To clean

To clean nylon icing bags, collars and connectors, squeeze out the surplus icing carefully. Do not apply too much pressure or the bag may burst. Wash in warm water with a little washing-up liquid then leave to soak overnight in warm water. Dry thoroughly before storing.

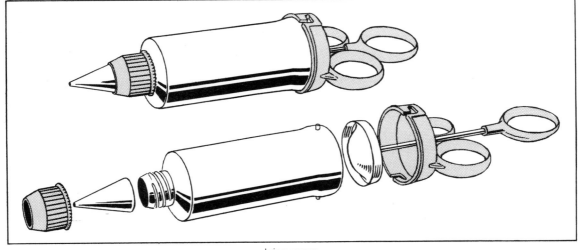

Icing pump

Icing pumps

Icing pumps are usually sold as part of an icing set, complete with nozzles. They are made of metal or polythene and consist of a large tube with screw-on nozzles at one end and a plunger with holes for two fingers and a thumb at the other. The plunger unscrews for easy refilling and the pump dismantles for easy cleaning.

The disadvantage of the icing pump is that you cannot 'feel' how the icing is reacting to the pressure applied to the plunger — this may result in too little or too much icing being pushed through the nozzle at the other end. Also, the consistency of the icing, must be correct for good results.

To clean

To clean the icing pump, dismantle it and scoop out any surplus icing. Wash thoroughly in warm water with a little washing-up liquid. Dry thoroughly before storing.

Turntables

If you intend to do lots of icing, especially formal celebration cakes covered in royal icing, then it is well worth investing in a precision-made metal icing turntable. These turntables stand about 15–20 cm (6–8 in) high and comprise a heavy base and a flat top which rotates. With the use of this type of turntable, all icing is simplified, especially icing the side of round cakes.

There is quite a technique in using a turntable to ice the side of a round cake in one movement:

1 Centre the cake and secure to the cake board with icing.
2 Position the cake on top of the turntable.
3 Spread the icing roughly over the side of the cake with a small palette knife, ensuring that the side is completely covered. Roughly level the side of the cake with a paddling action.
4 If right-handed, place the left hand as far around the back of the cake as you can comfortably reach and hold the underside of the turntable.
5 In the right hand, hold a small palette knife or icing comb (see page 12) upright and at an angle of 45° to the cake, as far around the

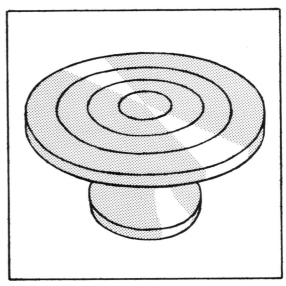

Metal icing turntable

back of the cake to meet and if possible to overlap slightly the other hand.

6 Move both hands towards the front of the cake, smoothing the side with the comb and turning the turntable to complete a full cycle.

Note If you are left-handed use the opposite hands.

A precision-made metal icing turntable is expensive and you may not feel able to buy one immediately. Look through your kitchen equipment and see how you can improvise. A large deep dinner plate or old fashioned soup plate turned upside down will move quite well on a smooth worktop surface. A polythene dumb waiter is ideal if used carefully, even though it is not as sturdy as a metal one.

The turntable is useful for royal icing as even a heavy cake can easily be moved when piping to check consistency of the design at all angles, especially when icing large formal cakes that are very heavy to keep lifting.

Icing rulers and combs

The top and side of a cake can be flat iced quite successfully with a long sturdy palette knife with a straight edge — at least as long as the width of the cake and ideally about 2·5 cm (1 in) longer. However, there are two pieces of equipment to make flat icing simpler.

The icing ruler looks like a conventional ruler without any markings. It is usually quite strong and will not bend unless great pressure is applied. The icing ruler is used to level the icing on the top of the cake. Hold it at an angle of 45° to the cake surface and pull towards you with as much even pressure as is needed to level the icing in one steady movement.

The icing comb is a piece of polythene about 12 cm (5 in) long and about 7 cm (3 in) wide. It has one straight edge and one edge shaped for easy holding. It is just the right depth for the side of the cake and is much easier to control than a long knife.

Hold the comb at 45° to the cake and move it around the side to smooth the surface. There is also a comb with a serrated edge which gives a very effective finish to the side of the cake (see page 91).

Icing templates

When planning a simple design for a formal cake, you can draw the design on a piece of greaseproof paper the same size as the cake

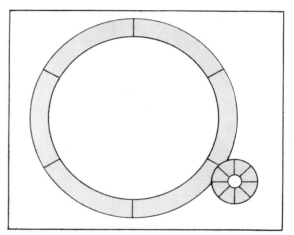

Circular icing templates

Long palette knife and icing ruler

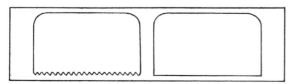

Straight- and serrated-edged icing combs

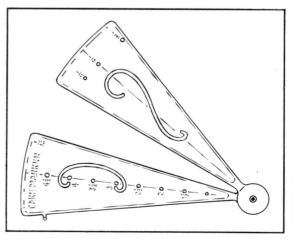

Triangular icing template

and then transfer to the top of the cake for piping guidelines. When planning a more complex design to be repeated in sections over the cake, an icing template is a useful piece of equipment. Icing templates are shaped pieces of metal or polythene either in the form of rings with quarter, sixth and eighth markings, or triangles. Both are used in the same way to ensure the design is spaced evenly over the top or sides of the cake. (See also page 35 for how to use a template.)

Icing nails and moulds

Icing nails look like upturned saucers of metal or polythene mounted on a nail. They are used as a rotating surface for piping flowers. A little icing is spread on the surface of the nail and a small square of non-stick or waxed paper is placed on top. The flower is then piped on to the paper, the nail being easily rotated as each petal is piped (see page 30).

You can improvise by pushing a bottle cork on to the point of a long clean nail or skewer and using it in exactly the same way.

Icing moulds are used when piping raised trellis work. The trellis lines are piped on to the

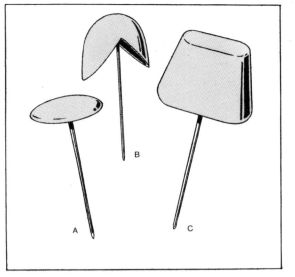

A icing nail; B and C icing moulds

mould and left to dry completely. The trellis shape is then lifted carefully from the mould and placed in position in the design on the cake. You can improvise by using upturned greased patty tins or barquette moulds.

Icing recipes

Royal icing

4 egg whites
900 g (2 lb) icing sugar, sifted
15 ml (1 tbsp) lemon juice
10 ml (2 tsp) glycerine

Whisk the egg whites in a bowl until slightly frothy. Stir in about a quarter of the icing sugar with a wooden spoon. Continue adding more sugar, beating well after each addition, until about three-quarters of the sugar has been added. Beat in the lemon juice and continue beating for about 10 minutes until the icing is smooth and meringue-like. Beat in the sugar until the right consistency is achieved — this will ensure an icing that is easy to handle. Stir in the glycerine, which helps prevent the icing from becoming too hard.

Note Do not add glycerine to the icing to be used on the bottom two tiers of a wedding cake.

For flat icing and writing
Stand the wooden spoon upright in the icing and it should fall slowly to one side.

For piping with star or shell nozzles
The icing should be a little stiffer than above — beat in a little more icing sugar.

For flooding
The icing should be thinner — beat in a little more egg white.

For peak icing (snow effect)
The icing should pull into well formed peaks with the back of the spoon.

Note You can make royal icing in an electric mixer but take care not to overbeat or the icing will become too fluffy, giving a rough surface, and will break if piped.

Once the icing is made, especially if made in an electric mixer, turn it into a polythene con-

tainer or bag. Cover and keep for 24 hours to allow the air bubbles to rise to the surface. Just before using, beat lightly and adjust the consistency if necessary.
Makes about 900 g (2 lb)

Almond paste

100 g (4 oz) icing sugar, sifted
100 g (4 oz) caster sugar
225 g (8 oz) ground almonds
5 ml (1 tsp) lemon juice
almond essence
1 egg or 2 egg yolks, beaten

Place both sugars in a bowl and stir in the ground almonds. Add the lemon juice, a few drops of essence and enough egg to bind to a firm but manageable dough. Turn on to a board dusted with sifted icing sugar and knead until smooth.
Makes about 450 g (1 lb)

Butter cream

225 g (8 oz) icing sugar
100 g (4 oz) butter
vanilla essence (or other flavouring)
15—30 ml (1—2 tbsp) milk or warm water

Sift the icing sugar into a bowl. Cream the butter until soft and gradually beat in the icing sugar, adding a few drops of essence and the milk or water.
This quantity is sufficient to coat the sides of a 20·5-cm (8-in) cake and provide a topping or a filling.

Note To coat the sides and provide a thicker topping and filling, increase the amounts of butter and sugar to 150 g (5 oz) and 275 g (10 oz) respectively.

VARIATIONS

Orange or lemon butter cream
Omit the vanilla essence and add a little finely grated orange or lemon rind and a little of the juice, beating well to avoid curdling the mixture.

Walnut butter cream
Stir 30 ml (2 level tbsp) finely chopped walnuts into the butter cream.

Almond butter cream
Stir 30 ml (2 level tbsp) very finely chopped toasted almonds into the butter cream.

Coffee butter cream
Omit the vanilla essence and flavour with 10 ml (2 level tsp) instant coffee powder dissolved in some of the heated liquid. Alternatively, use 15 ml (1 tbsp) coffee essence to replace an equal amount of the liquid.

Chocolate butter cream
Flavour either by adding 25—40 g (1—1½ oz) melted chocolate, omitting 15 ml (1 tbsp) liquid, or by adding 15 ml (1 level tbsp) cocoa powder dissolved in a little hot water (this should be cooled before adding to the mixture).

Mocha butter cream
Dissolve 5 ml (1 level tsp) cocoa powder and 10 ml (2 level tsp) instant coffee powder in a little warm water taken from the measured amount; cool before adding to the mixture.

White praline

75 g (3 oz) granulated sugar
60 ml (4 tbsp) water
pinch cream of tartar
25 g (1 oz) blanched almonds, chopped

Heat the sugar and water, stirring until the sugar is dissolved. Boil for 1—2 minutes without colouring the syrup. Add the cream of tartar and almonds; immediately pour into an oiled tin and leave to set. Lift the set praline and place between two sheets of greaseproof paper. Crush finely with a rolling pin. Sieve the praline and crush any larger pieces.
   White praline has been used to decorate the cake on page 54.

Note For golden praline, brown the almonds and boil the syrup until golden brown.

Kneaded fondant icing

450 g (1 lb) icing sugar
1 egg white
50 g (2 oz) liquid glucose
colouring
flavouring

Making kneaded fondant icing

Sift the icing sugar into a mixing bowl and make a well in the centre. Add the egg white and glucose. Beat, gradually drawing the icing sugar into the centre of the bowl, until the mixture is quite stiff. Knead the icing, incorporating any remaining icing sugar, until smooth and manageable. Add colouring and flavouring and a little more icing sugar if necessary.

This icing can be stored in a sealed polythene bag or container in a cool place.
Makes about 450 g (1 lb)

Glacé icing

100–175 g (4–6 oz) icing sugar, sifted
15–30 ml (1–2 tbsp) warm water
flavouring

Place the icing sugar in a bowl and gradually add the water until the icing is thick enough to coat the back of a spoon. Stir in the chosen flavouring.

If necessary, add more sugar or water to obtain the correct consistency. Add a few drops of colouring if required and use at once.

For icing of a finer texture, place the sugar, water and flavouring in a small pan and heat, stirring, until the mixture is warm — do not make it too hot. The icing should coat the back of a wooden spoon and look smooth and glossy.

This quantity is sufficient to cover the top of a 20·5-cm (8-in) cake or about 18 small cakes.

VARIATIONS

Orange icing
Substitute 15–30 ml (1–2 tbsp) strained orange juice for the measured water.

Lemon icing
Substitute 15 ml (1 tbsp) strained lemon juice for the same amount of measured water.

Chocolate icing
Blend 10 ml (2 level tsp) cocoa powder in a little hot water and use to replace the same amount of measured water.

Coffee icing
Flavour with either 5 ml (1 tsp) coffee essence or 10 ml (2 level tsp) instant coffee powder, dissolved in a little of the heated measured water.

Mocha icing
Flavour with 5 ml (1 level tsp) cocoa powder and 10 ml (2 level tsp) instant coffee powder, dissolved in a little of the heated measured water.

Liqueur icing
Replace 10–15 ml (2–3 tsp) of the measured water by a chosen liqueur.

American frosting

450 g (1 lb) granulated or caster sugar
120 ml (8 tbsp) water
pinch cream of tartar
2 egg whites

In a small pan, gently heat the sugar in the water with the cream of tartar added, stirring until dissolved. Then, without stirring, boil to 120°C (240°F). Whisk the egg whites stiffly. Remove the sugar syrup from the heat and immediately the bubbles subside, pour on to the egg white in a thin stream; whisk the mixture continuously. When the frosting thickens, shows signs of going dull round the edges and is almost cold, pour it quickly over the cake and at once spread evenly or mark into swirls with a palette knife. *This quantity is sufficient to cover the top and sides of a 23-cm (9-in) cake.*

Note To make this frosting correctly, it is necessary to use a sugar-boiling thermometer. If you do not possess one, you can make Seven minute frosting (see below) — this has to be eaten within 24 hours.

VARIATIONS

Orange frosting
Add a few drops of orange essence and a little orange food colouring to the mixture while whisking and before the frosting thickens.

Lemon frosting
Add a little lemon juice while whisking the mixture.

Caramel frosting
Substitute demerara sugar for the white sugar; follow the same method as above.

Coffee frosting
Add 10 ml (2 tsp) coffee essence to the mixture while whisking.

Seven minute frosting

This is an imitation American frosting that does not need a thermometer. It must be eaten within 24 hours.

2 egg whites
325 g (12 oz) caster sugar
pinch salt
60 ml (4 tbsp) water
pinch cream of tartar

Put all the ingredients into a bowl and whisk lightly. Place the bowl over hot water and continue whisking for about 7 minutes until the mixture thickens sufficiently to hold 'peaks'. Timing depends on the whisk used and the heat of the water.
This quantity is sufficient to cover the top and sides of a 23-cm (9-in) cake.

Note The same variations can be made as for American frosting.

Making American frosting

Techniques of almond paste

Applying almond paste to a square cake

Almond paste is usually applied to the top and sides of a cake. If the top of the cake is not very level, turn the cake upside down. Alternatively, if the cake has risen the top can be trimmed to level it.

Measure the length of one side of the cake with a piece of string and cut it.

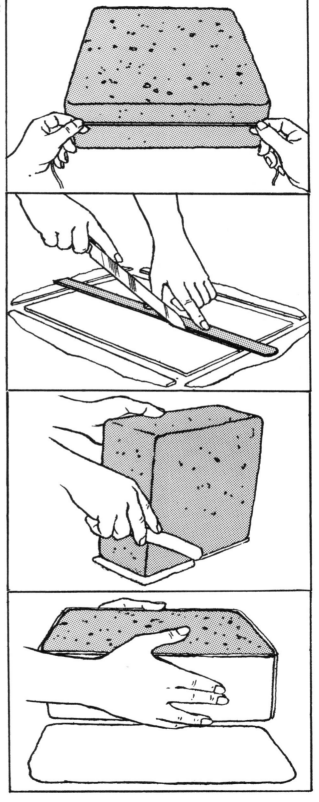

Use two-thirds of the almond paste for the sides. Divide into two equal pieces. Roll out each piece on a surface dusted with sifted icing sugar to a rectangle the length of the string and twice the depth of the cake. Trim the edges using a knife and icing ruler for a straight edge then cut each rectangle in half lengthways. Knead the trimmings into the remaining third of the almond paste and roll into a square to fit the top of the cake.

Brush one side of the cake with apricot glaze. Turn the cake on its side with the glazed side down and hold it firmly between both palms. Place the glazed edge on one piece of almond paste, making sure the intended top edge of the cake is square with the almond paste. Trim away the ends and mould any surplus almond paste into the base of the cake. Repeat, covering the other three sides. Roll a clean straight-sided jam jar around the sides of the cake, keeping the corners square.

Brush the top of the cake with apricot glaze. Either lift the almond paste on to the cake over a rolling pin, carefully seal the edges and roll lightly with a rolling pin, or leave the almond paste on a surface well dusted with sifted icing sugar and turn the cake on to the almond paste. Trim away any surplus almond paste. Slide the cake towards you on to a board and turn the right side up. Leave to dry for 1–2 days or ideally a week before icing.

Applying almond paste to a round cake

If the top of the cake is not very level turn the cake upside down. Alternatively, if the cake has risen the top can be trimmed to level it.

Measure round the side of the cake with a piece of string or thread and cut it where the string meets.

For the side of the cake, roll out two-thirds of the almond paste, on a surface dusted with sifted icing sugar, to a rectangle half the length of the string and twice the depth of the cake. Trim the edges using a knife and icing ruler for a straight edge then cut the rectangle in half lengthways. Knead the trimmings into the remaining third of the almond paste and roll into a round to fit the top of the cake.

Brush the side of the cake with apricot glaze. Holding the cake firmly between both palms, turn the cake on its side. Roll the cake along the strips of almond paste, making sure the intended top edge of the cake is square with the almond paste. Use a round-bladed knife to smooth the two joins, then mould any surplus almond paste into the base of the cake. Roll a clean straight-sided jam jar around the side of the cake.

Brush the top of the cake with apricot glaze. Either lift the almond paste on to the cake over a rolling pin, carefully seal the edges and lightly roll with the rolling pin, or leave the round of almond paste on a surface well dusted with sifted icing sugar and turn the cake on to the almond paste. Trim away the surplus almond paste. Slide the cake towards you on to a board and turn the right side up. Leave to dry for 1–2 days or ideally a week before icing.

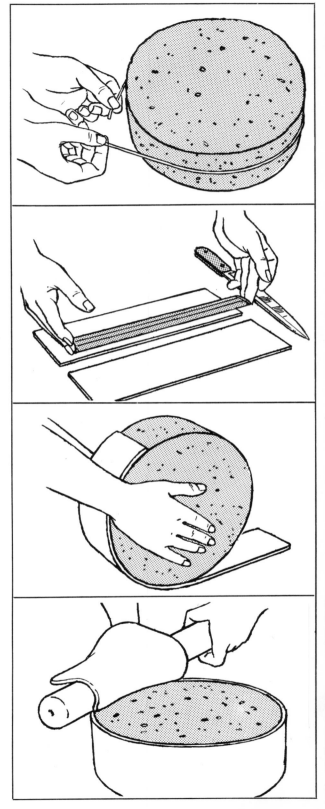

Techniques of base icing

Applying royal icing

It is easier to apply royal icing in two stages or three if a square cake — two opposite sides at a time. Apply the icing to the sides or top first and leave to dry for about 24 hours before icing the other surface.

Place a small spoonful of icing on the cake board, place the cake on top, making sure it is in the centre of the board. Stand the cake and board on a non-slip surface. Spoon almost half the icing on to the top of the cake and spread it evenly over the surface with a palette knife, using a paddling action to remove any air bubbles that may remain. Using an icing ruler or palette knife longer than the width of the cake, without applying any pressure, draw it steadily across the top of the cake at an angle of 30°, to smooth the surface. Neaten the edges with a palette knife, removing any surplus icing. For best results, leave to dry for about 24 hours before applying the icing to the side of the cake.

To make icing the side of a cake easier, place it on an icing turntable. Spread the remaining icing on the side of the cake and smooth it roughly with a small palette knife, using a paddling action. Hold the palette knife or icing comb upright and at an angle of 45° to the cake. Draw the knife or comb towards you to smooth the surface (see page 12). For a square cake apply icing to each side separately. Neaten the edges with a palette knife, removing any surplus icing.

For a really smooth finish, apply a second thinner coat of icing, allowing the first coat to dry for 1–2 days first. Use fine sandpaper to sand down any imperfections or slight marks in the first coat. Brush the surface of the cake with a greasefree pastry brush to remove the icing dust.

A simple yet effective finish for the sides of a cake is to 'rib' it with a serrated icing comb. Spread the icing on the side of the cake and smooth it roughly with a palette knife. Hold the icing comb upright and at an angle of 45° to the cake. Draw the comb around the sides of the cake without pressing the points of the comb into the almond paste. For a two-tone colour effect, flat ice the side of the cake in a coloured icing and leave to dry for 24–48 hours. Apply a coat of white icing on top and comb with a serrated icing comb. The coloured icing will then be revealed through the white icing (see page 91).

The cake board can also be covered with icing. This is usually very effective if the cake is iced in a pastel colour. Once the side of the cake is completely dry, spread a thin layer of icing over the board with a palette knife. Holding the knife at an angle, smooth the icing in one movement by turning the turntable as above.

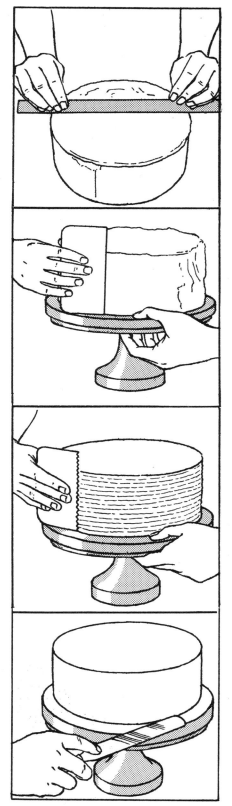

Applying American frosting

American frosting sets very quickly so collect the necessary equipment for applying the icing — palette knife, tablespoon or spatula before starting to make the icing. Also have the cake, cake board and any decorations near to hand. Once the icing is made, place a small spoonful on the cake board and place the cake on top, making sure it is in the centre of the board. Spoon all the icing on to the centre of the cake.

Work very quickly as the icing will soon start to set. Using a palette knife, spread the icing over the surface of the top and sides of the cake, making sure the cake is completely covered.

Using the back of a small metal spoon, quickly mark the icing into well formed swirls all over the cake. Do not try to peak the icing as you would royal icing as the icing will come away from the cake.

If simple decorations are to be added, quickly place in position on the cake while the icing is still soft and leave to set. The icing forms a crisp crust but underneath it will remain soft and marshmallow-like.

Applying kneaded fondant icing

Place a small spoonful of jam or royal icing on the cake board and place the cake in the centre of the board. Measure the size of the top and sides of the cake with a piece of string. Knead the fondant icing until pliable on a surface dusted with sifted icing sugar. Roll out the fondant icing in one piece, roughly the shape of the cake i.e. round or square, until a little larger than the length of the string.

Brush the surface of the cake with beaten egg white if the cake is covered with almond paste, or with apricot glaze if applying the icing straight on to the cake surface. Lift the fondant icing on to a rolling pin and place on top of the cake. Unroll the icing allowing it to drape over the cake.

For a round cake, trim away the excess icing that forms folds in the icing with a pair of scissors. Mould the icing into the sides of the cake with the hands until the seams can no longer be seen. For a square cake, trim away the excess icing at the four corners. Mould the icing where it is cut into the sides of the cake as above.

Mould the icing around the top edge of the cake to form a right angled edge. Trim the excess icing from the base edge of the cake with a sharp knife. Knead clean trim-mings into one piece and mould into cake decorations (see pages 36–38), or place in a sealed polythene container or bag and store in a cool place until ready to use. Leave the cake to dry for about 24 hours before decorating with piped icing.

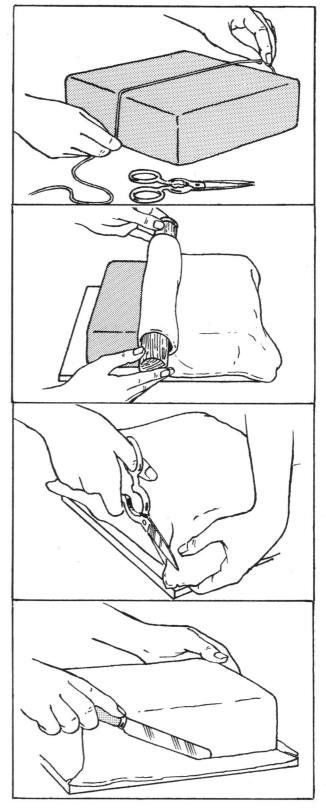

Applying glacé icing

Place the cake on a wire rack with a plate or clean baking sheet underneath to catch any surplus icing. Collect together any decorations such as glacé cherries, nuts, silver balls, etc.

When icing the top and sides of the cake, pour the icing on to the centre of the cake and spread it right to the edge of the cake with a palette knife. Allow the icing to run down the sides evenly, fill any spaces with surplus icing either left in the bowl or from the plate underneath the cake. Take care not to include any cake crumbs.

When using a thicker icing and only the top of the cake is to be covered, a grease-proof collar can be used. Cut a piece of greaseproof paper the depth of the cake plus 2·5 cm (1 in). Wrap it tightly round the side of the cake and secure with a paper clip. Pour the icing on to the cake and spread it almost to the greaseproof collar. Allow the icing to set before removing the collar.

Place simple decorations in position when the icing has stopped flowing and a slight skin has formed. If decorations are added when the icing is too wet they will slide off the cake; if added when the icing is completely set the surface will crack and spoil the icing. Leave for about an hour to allow the icing to set completely. The same method can be used to decorate small cakes, although it is sometimes quicker and easier to dip the top of each cake into the icing.

Applying butter cream

For a sandwich or larger cake, spread a little of the butter cream evenly over the underside of both cakes with a round-bladed knife, smoothing it right to the edges. Place one on top of the other and press down gently. The two cakes will not slide apart when cutting if sandwiched together in this way.

Spread the sides of the cake roughly with butter cream. Using a round-bladed knife held upright, draw the knife towards you at an angle of 45° to smooth the surface. Turn the cake on its side, hold between the palms of the hands and roll the sides in chopped nuts, chocolate vermicelli or coconut.

Spoon more of the butter cream on top of the cake and spread smoothly and evenly to the edges of the cake, covering the surface completely. Move the knife in a paddling action to allow any air bubbles to come to the surface and then smooth level.

Pattern the surface with the prongs of a fork, or make pronounced paddle marks with a round-bladed knife. If wished, pipe a decorative border with an icing bag fitted with an eight point star nozzle and decorate with nuts, glacé cherries, angelica or chocolate drops.

Techniques of piping

Good results in piping can only be achieved with plenty of practice, using icing of the correct consistency. Royal icing and butter cream can be expensive materials to practise with, particularly as they dry and skin so quickly, preventing you from using them again. Therefore, simple instant mashed potato is cheap to produce, can be used many times and is of the right consistency. If you are a beginner, in the early stages try piping shell edges, rosettes and decorative borders with a large vegetable star or shell nozzle, using mashed potato on a clean surface — it can be spooned up and used time and time again.

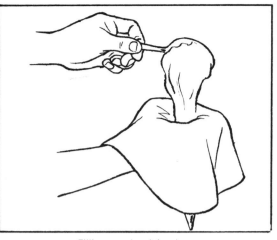
Filling a nylon icing bag

Consistency of icing

Glacé icing used for piping should be stiffer than the icing used to coat the top and sides of a cake. This can be used for piping lines — straight or curved.

Royal icing varies according to the type of piping. For dots, rosettes, shell edge, etc. the icing should be stiff enough to pull into well formed peaks in the bowl. For piping lines, the icing should be a little slacker but at the same time able to hold its shape (see page 25).

Butter cream should be stiff enough to leave well formed marks when a fork is pulled across the icing in the bowl. This can be used for piping rosettes, stars and shell edging.

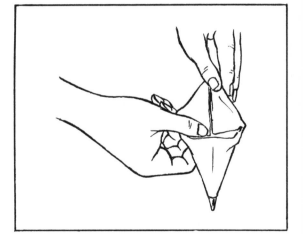
Closing a greaseproof icing bag

Filling icing bags

Even when working on a large cake with lots of piping in the design, it is better to use small icing bags and refill them rather than use one large bag. Icing is easier to control in small amounts because you don't need too much pressure to push the icing through the bag.

Place the nozzle in the icing bag and hold it loosely in one hand. Scoop a small amount of icing with a palette knife or teaspoon and place it in the base of the bag. Fill to two-thirds full, pushing the icing well down.

Fold the greaseproof icing bag over at the top, pushing the icing further into the bag at the same time, taking care not to squeeze the icing out of the top of the bag.

Holding a greaseproof icing bag

Open the hand and place the icing bag across the palm of the hand. Place the thumb on the cushion of folded paper at the top of the bag.

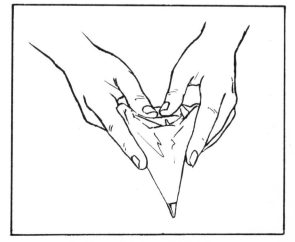
Holding a greaseproof icing bag

Fold over the four fingers and apply a steady even pressure until the icing begins to come out of the nozzle.

Holding a nylon icing bag

Place the thumb and forefinger around the icing in a nylon icing bag and twist tightly two or three times. This stops the icing squeezing out of the top of the bag when pressure is applied.

Open the hand and place the icing bag across the palm of the hand. Clasp the bag where it is twisted with the thumb and forefinger and maintain an even grip. Fold over the other three fingers and apply a steady but even pressure until the icing begins to come out of the nozzle. Wipe the icing away from the nozzle and you are ready to start piping.

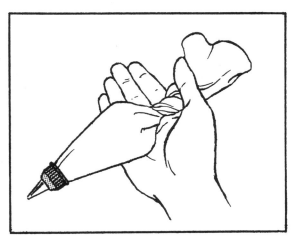

1. Holding a nylon icing bag

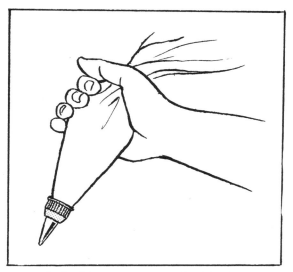

2. Applying pressure to a nylon icing bag

Note Royal icing will dry out quite quickly, so it is best to keep the filled icing bags in a polythene bag or covered with cling film. Also keep the bowl of icing covered with a clean damp cloth or cling film when not in use.

How to use a plain nozzle

Place a plain nozzle (No. 1, 2 or 3) in the icing bag and fill it with icing as above. Make sure the tip of the nozzle is wiped clean and completely free from icing or you will not be able to start the piping neatly.

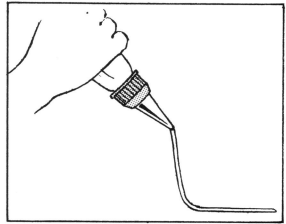

Piping a straight line

Piping a straight line Place the tip of the nozzle where the straight line is to begin. Apply slight pressure to the icing bag and as the icing starts to come from the nozzle, lift the icing bag about 2·5 cm (1 in) above the surface. This allows even the shakiest of hands to pipe a perfectly straight line. Move the hand in the direction of the line, guiding the icing bag with the other hand if wished, allowing the icing to flow evenly. When you reach about 1 cm ($\frac{1}{2}$ in) before the end of the line,

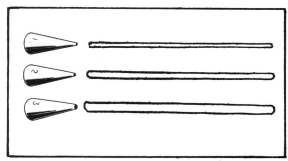

stop squeezing the icing bag and gently lower the tip of the nozzle to the surface. This action will end the line neatly. If you continued to squeeze the icing bag your line would end with an unwanted blob.

Piping trellis icing Once you can pipe straight lines you can then start trellis work. Pipe a series of parallel, straight lines in one direction over the area of the cake to be covered. Turn the cake and pipe another layer of parallel straight lines over the top of the first layer.

This idea can be developed further to create very interesting and effective designs. See the cakes on pages 83 and 92 for ideas.

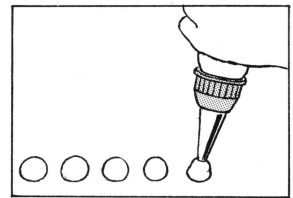

Piping dots

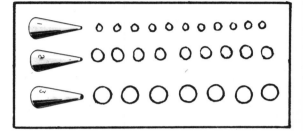

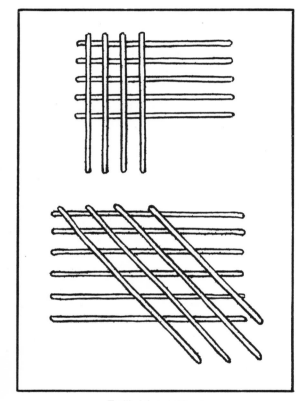

Trellis icing patterns

achieved by moving the nozzle in a circular motion or using a larger nozzle.

Piping curved lines Once you have control of the icing flowing from the nozzle, you can progress to piping curved lines and loops.

Make a template (see page 35), draw a series of even sized scallops on a piece of greaseproof paper or thin cardboard and use for practising. Place the tip of the nozzle at the beginning of the line and squeeze out a little icing. Lift the nozzle and allow the line to drape along the curve of the scallop. Lower the nozzle back to the surface as you reach the join between each scallop.

Piping dots The pressure required on the icing bag to pipe a dot is quite slight. Place the tip of the nozzle on the surface and hold the bag almost upright. Squeeze the icing bag gently and at the same time lift the nozzle slightly. Stop squeezing the icing bag, move the nozzle slightly in a gentle shaking action to avoid a 'tail' and lift the nozzle. Practise piping rows of different size dots. A larger dot can be

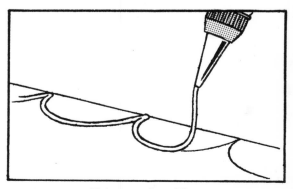

Piping a scalloped line

This will need plenty of practice before you can incorporate it sucessfully in the design of a cake (see page 72).

Piping patterns with dots and lines Simple but effective patterns can be created by combining dots and straight lines or loops.

Pipe a double row of even shaped dots spaced alternately. Pipe straight lines between the dots, using the centre of each dot as the point to begin and end each line.

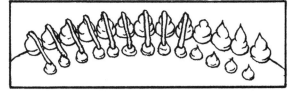

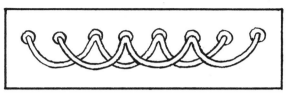

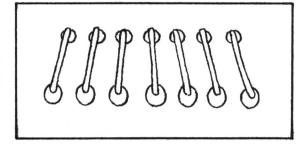

A simple edging for the base of a cake can be made by piping one row of dots actually on the side of the cake and a second row of dots on the cake board. Pipe lines between the two rows of dots taking the lines either straight down or diagonally to one side of the starting point.

All these designs are really effective if iced in either two contrasting colours or in darker and lighter shades of the same colour.

Writing Use any of the plain nozzles. Practise with simple capital letters to start with, using a plain nozzle (No. 3) and piping straight lines. The letters can be drawn on greaseproof paper and pricked out on to the icing surface with a pin. These letters can be piped like a series of straight lines ending each without a blob.

Once you can control the icing bag, progress to fancier writing. Books and magazines always prove a useful source for stylised lettering.

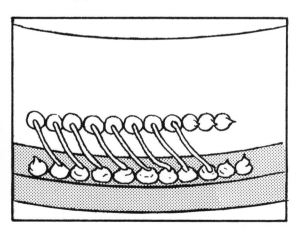

This edging can also be used on the top of the cake if the outside edge is built up enough to give a drop to the surface of the cake — you will need two tiers of dots on the outside edge and a single dot inside.

Another effective edging can be made by piping a single line of dots along the top edge of the cake. Pipe overlapping loops to alternate dots.

Piping plain and fancy writing

How to use a star nozzle

Star nozzles vary in the size of the tip of the nozzle, which determines the size of the piped star or rosette, and in the number of points to the star. Select a five or eight point star to begin with and then progress to the larger and more complex nozzles.

Piping a star Place a five or eight point star nozzle in the icing bag and fill it with icing of the correct consistency.

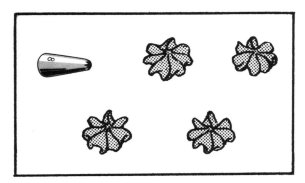

Hold the icing bag upright and just above the surface of the cake. Squeeze the icing from the bag. Stop squeezing once the star is formed on the surface and lift the nozzle away sharply. A good star should sit reasonably squat on the surface of the cake and not be 'lifted' up into a point. Practise until a perfect star is achieved.

Piping a rosette A rosette is piped with the same nozzle but the pipe is moved in a circular motion – like piping a large dot.

Hold the icing bag upright and just above the surface of the cake, squeeze gently and move the nozzle in a complete circle enclosing the middle. Pull the nozzle sharply away from the rosette without forming a point or tail.

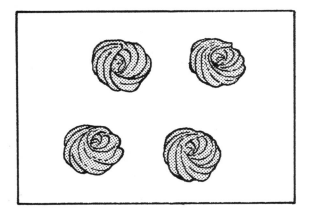

Piping a shell A shell edging can be made either with a star nozzle or with a special shell nozzle – the movement of the nozzle is the same. The shell nozzle will give a fatter, fuller shell than the star nozzle with more ridges.

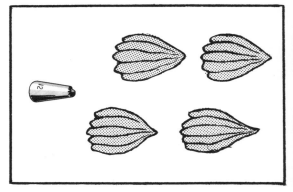

Hold the icing bag at an angle to the surface and just above it. Squeeze the icing bag until the icing begins to come from the nozzle and a head is formed. Pull the icing bag gently to the right and at the same time release the pressure on the bag. The shell should be well formed and come to a neat point.

A shell border is achieved by piping a series of well formed shells together, linked in a line. Each shell should be quite distinct in its shape with a head and pointed tail. Many beginners pipe a shell edge without releasing the pressure to form the point and the result is a very bulky edge which is not even in size.

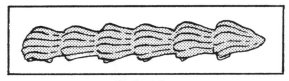

Shell edging

Piping patterns with a star or shell nozzle An effective border can be made with either the star or shell nozzle piped in a continuous line, moving it from side to side at the same time to give a zig-zag effect. You may need to stop in the middle of the line to turn the cake. This can easily be disguised if care is taken in matching the pattern at the join.

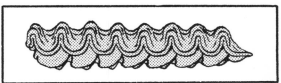

An *alternating shell edge* can be piped on the top edge of the cake so the head of one shell is piped on the top and the head of the next shell is on the side of the cake. Repeat at the base so one shell is on the cake board and the other on the side of the cake.

A *twisted rope* effect can be achieved with the star nozzle by piping a continuous line of overlapping circles.

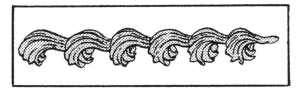

.We have used a three point star nozzle for several designs that appear in the book (see page 93). This produces a neat *trefoil* and can be piped either way up, but keep the nozzle in the same position throughout the design. Use in exactly the same way as for the star nozzle.

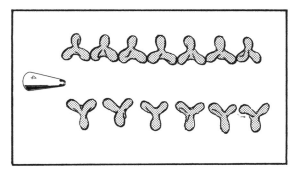

A simple *scroll* edging can be made with either the star or shell nozzle. If the scrolls are to be well spaced they are better planned with the use of a template (see page 35). If they are closely spaced they can be piped straight on to the cake.

Squeeze the icing from the nozzle evenly to make sure the scroll is the same thickness along its length.

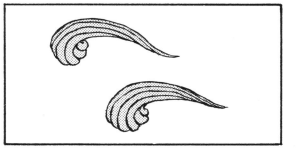

A scroll can be used as part of a design for the top of the cake.

How to use a basket nozzle

The basket nozzle is a thick ribbon nozzle with one or both edges serrated. It is flattened at the tip to produce a ribbon of ridged icing.

Piping basket work You need one icing bag fitted with the basket nozzle and one fitted with a plain nozzle (No. 2 or 3).

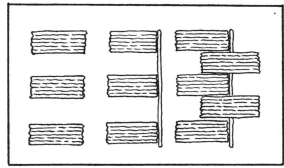

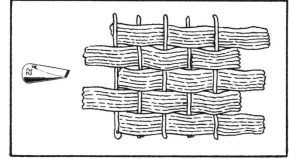

Hold the basket nozzle sideways to the cake and at an angle, and pipe three short lines the same length evenly spaced apart, one above the other. Pipe a straight vertical line along the edge of the basket icing. Pipe three more lines of the same length, starting in between the first basket lines and coming over the straight line.

A *pleated ribbon* edge can be made with a

basket nozzle. Move the nozzle in a backwards/forwards motion to form even spaced pleats.

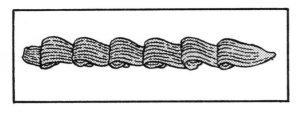

How to use a petal nozzle

This nozzle is only used for making flowers and some leaves. It is easier to pipe the flowers on to a piece of non-stick or waxed paper on an icing nail. When you become really skilled, you can pipe some flowers in position directly on to the cake.

Piping a rose Place a little icing on the top of the icing nail and stick a small square of non-stick or waxed paper on top. Place the petal nozzle in an icing bag and half fill with icing — it is easier to work with small quantities of icing. Hold the petal nozzle with the thin part uppermost. Pipe a cone of icing, twisting the nail between the thumb and forefinger, to form the centre of the rose. Pipe five or six petals around the centre of the rose, overlapping each and piping the outer petals so they are more open and lie flatter.

Lift the square of paper from the nail and leave the rose for about 24 hours until completely dry, before using.

Vary the shape of the roses by adding as many or few petals as you wish.

Using the petal nozzle needs practice, but once you have mastered the movements you can make other flowers.

For a daisy Work with the thick edge of the nozzle to the centre and pipe five even sized petals.

A few piped flowers can be added as an extra decoration in the design of a cake (see

Piping a daisy on an icing nail

page 74) or they can form a major part of the design by being used in their own right instead of a piped border (see page 92).

Leaves can be piped using a greaseproof icing bag. Make up the bag as normal and fill with icing without a nozzle before snipping off the top. Cut the tip of the bag to a point.

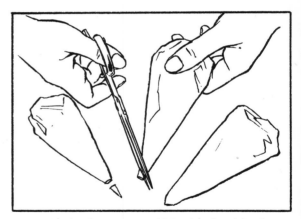

Cutting the tip of a greaseproof icing bag for piping leaves

Squeeze the bag until the icing comes from the tip. Move the icing bag sideways in three overlapping movements. For the third movement

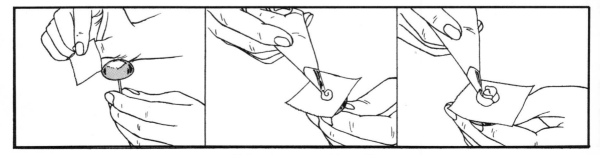

Piping a rose on an icing nail

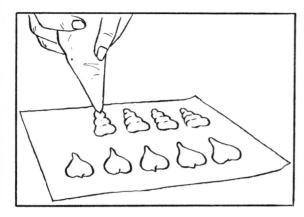

pull the bag away quickly to form a point. A leaf nozzle, the same shape as the snipped bag, is available.

It is easier to pipe leaves straight on to the cake, but if preferred, pipe them on to a piece of non-stick or waxed paper first and leave to dry for 24 hours before positioning on the cake.

Piping leaves using a greaseproof icing bag

Techniques of run-out

Run-out cake decorations were once made only by highly skilled bakers, confectioners and caterers. The techniques have been simplified to bring this very attractive form of cake decorating within everyone's capabilities.

A run-out is a shaped piece of icing—for example a plaque, letter, number, flower, leaf, face or animal. The outline of a simple shape is piped straight on to the surface of the cake and then flooded with icing. For more complex shapes, it is easier and more usual to pipe the outline of the shape on to a piece of non-stick or waxed paper then flood with icing. Once completely dry, the paper is peeled off and the shape is transferred to the cake.

Equipment
Very little equipment is required for run-outs. Besides an icing bag with a plain nozzle, you will need a small skewer, cocktail stick or fine artist's paint brush, a pencil and non-stick or waxed paper.

How to do run-outs

1 Select the shape or shapes you want to make.
2 Using a pencil, draw the outline of the shape on to a piece of cardboard or thick paper and then place a piece of non-stick or waxed paper over the top. Hold in position with a dot of icing at each corner of the cardboard.
3 Using an icing bag fitted with a plain nozzle (No. 2), pipe (trace) a continuous line of icing following the outline of the shape. Move the

non-stick or waxed paper along over the card and repeat if duplicate shapes are required, or use more than one pattern.
4 Using a plain nozzle (No. 3) or a teaspoon and slightly thinner icing, pipe or spoon the icing into the centre of the shape — this is known as flooding. Using the skewer, cocktail stick or fine paint brush, ease the icing into all the corners. Fill the centre of the run-out with enough icing to give a slightly domed shape. For very large areas, it is easier to spoon the icing into the shape.

Always make more run-outs than required to allow for breakages.
5 Leave for 1–2 days until completely dry.
6 To remove the paper from large run-outs, place on the edge of a worktop or board. Pull the paper downwards, sliding the run-out towards you at the same time. This will gently ease the paper from the back of the run-out. For smaller shapes, turn them over and carefully peel off the paper.
7 Pipe in lines or dots to complete the detail of the run-out or paint in any details with diluted food colouring.
8 Place in position on the cake design and secure with a little icing.

Run-out writing Writing on a cake can be given more depth if each letter in the word is run-out separately. This can either be done straight on to the cake, see the christening cake on page 95, or piped separately on to a piece of paper and added when dry, see the anniversary cake on page 91.

Draw or trace the letters of the words on a piece of non-stick or waxed paper. Using an icing bag fitted with a plain nozzle (No. 1 or 2), pipe around the outline of each letter. Flood the sections of each letter and leave to dry for 1—2 days. Remove the paper, pipe a little icing on the back of each letter and place in position on the cake. Alternatively, if the lettering is to be piped straight on to the cake, draw the letters on a piece of greaseproof paper. Place the paper in position on the cake and prick around the outline of each letter with a pin. Remove the paper and continue as above.

Run-outs can be stored and will keep well for many months without discolouring. Wrap each piece in tissue paper or cotton wool and pack carefully in an airtight container.

Flowers

Run-out flowers can be used to decorate a simple Victoria sandwich or on a formal iced cake.

You will need:
coloured royal icing
yellow royal icing
food colouring

Draw the outline of the flower on several pieces of non-stick or waxed paper.

Using an icing bag fitted with a plain nozzle (No. 2) and chosen coloured icing, pipe around the outline of each petal.

Flood thinner icing into each petal, easing the icing into the corners with a skewer or fine paint brush. Leave to dry for 1—2 days before removing from the paper. Pipe an outline around each petal. Using the yellow icing, pipe stamens into the centre of each flower. A little diluted food colouring can be painted on to the flower petals. For a more realistic effect, paint darker colouring in the centre of the flower and paler colouring towards the outer edges of the petals.

White bells

Used for decoration on the Christmas ring cake on page 102 but also suitable for a wedding cake.

You will need:
white royal icing
silver balls

Draw the outline of ten bells on pieces of non-stick or waxed paper. Pipe around the outline of the shape with a plain nozzle (No. 2). Flood the centres with slightly thinner white icing and leave to dry for 1—2 days. Remove the bells from the paper and pipe a single line around the outline of each bell. Pipe three small dots at the base of each and place a silver ball on top of each dot.

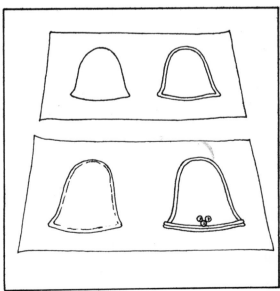

Hand-made decorations (*pages 36—47*)

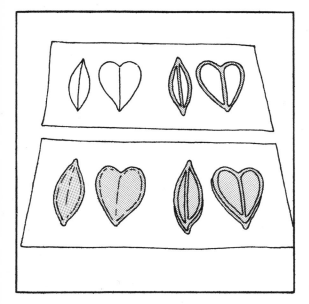

Leaves

Holly leaves are used on the Christmas cake on page 101.

You will need:
green royal icing
green food colouring

Draw the outline of the chosen leaves on pieces of non-stick or waxed paper. Draw a vertical line down the centre of each leaf. Using an icing bag fitted with a plain nozzle (No. 1 or 2), pipe around the outline of each leaf and down the centre line. Using the same icing bag, flood the two halves of each leaf separately, easing the icing into the corners with a skewer or cocktail stick. Leave to dry completely for 24 hours. Colour a little icing a slightly darker green and use to pipe in the veins of the leaves. Leave to dry for about 24 hours before carefully removing from the paper.

Lace edging

Although not strictly run-out work, piped lace work makes a very attractive edging for a cake — see the christening cake on page 95.

You will need:
white royal icing
silver balls

Draw the outline of the lace on a piece of cardboard or thick paper. Place under a large piece of non-stick or waxed paper. Move the template under the paper for each piece of lace. Using an icing bag fitted with a plain nozzle (No. 1 or 2), pipe in the five evenly spaced loops just touching each other. Once you can pipe with confidence, pipe the lace freehand. Leave to dry for a few minutes and then pipe a small dot at the peak of the centre three loops. Leave to dry for 1—2 days before very carefully peeling away the paper.

Chocolate and mandarin cake (*page 56*),
Orange and coconut sandwich cake (*page 53*),
Coffee and walnut sandwich cake (*page 55*),
Coffee and chocolate loaf (*page 58*)

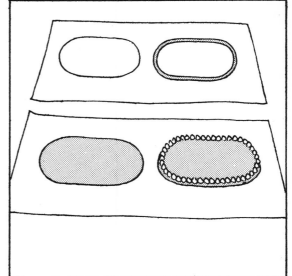

Numbers or letters

You will need:
white royal icing

Draw the outline of the required numbers or letters on a piece of non-stick or waxed paper. Using an icing bag fitted with a plain nozzle (No. 2), pipe around the outline of each number.

Thin the icing slightly and use to flood between the lines of each number or letter. Ease the icing into the corners with a fine paint brush or skewer. Leave to dry before removing from the paper.

Note Always make extra numbers or letters in case of breakage.

Plaques

You will need:
white royal icing
food colourings

Draw the outline of the shape of the plaque required — round, oval, square or rectangular. Using an icing bag fitted with a plain nozzle (No. 2) and the coloured icing of your choice, pipe around the outline. Thin the icing slightly and use to flood the centre of the plaque. Leave to dry for at least 24 hours before removing from the paper.

Using an icing bag fitted with a plain nozzle (No. 2), pipe small dots around the outside edge of the plaque in the same or contrasting colour. If liked, you can mount run-out letters or numbers on the plaque or paint a small picture or design with food colouring before piping the dots around the edge.

Making and using a template

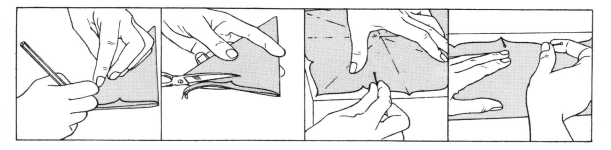

Once you have mastered flat icing, piping and run-out work, you are ready to design and ice a complete cake. For your first cake it is better to pipe a simple design perfectly. Think about the design and draw it out roughly on a piece of paper as a guide. If the design includes shaped lines then it is better to make a pattern or template. The template can be made from thin cardboard or greaseproof paper. Cut a piece the size of the top of the cake and draw or trace the chosen design. Place the template on top of the flat iced cake and mark the outline of the design by pricking through the card with a pin. Lift the template and the outline of the design will be clearly marked on the surface of the cake. You can also use a template in the same way if the design on the side of the cake is quite intricate or precise. It is much easier to make and use a template to mark scallops on the side of a cake, particularly a round cake. Look at the christening cake on page 94 and the illustrations will show you how the design was achieved.

Step 1 Cut a square piece of paper the exact size of the top of the cake. Fold the paper into quarters and then fold the small square of paper in half to make a triangle. Draw the shaped scallop on the top piece of paper with a pencil.

Step 2 Cut along the line exactly with a pair of scissors. Open out the paper and place it on top of the cake. Secure it in position with a number of pins.

Step 3 Use another pin to prick a line around the outline of the scallops. Remove the paper from the top and you will have the design marked on the top of the cake.

Step 4 Fold the piece of paper in half and use in exactly the same way to mark the design on the side of the cake.

You now have clear guide lines to follow and the piping can be completed without any difficulty but do make sure that your piping covers the pin pricks in the flat icing completely.

Hand-made decorations
Modelling with kneaded fondant icing

Kneaded fondant icing is also known as Australian fondant icing, plastic icing, or modelling, cold or uncooked fondant. Do not confuse this icing with the traditional boiled fondant, that is made by a more complex method and less pliable for modelling.

Fondant icing is a simple icing made from icing sugar, liquid glucose or glucose syrup and egg white. The glucose helps to produce an icing that is quite pliable and easy to handle and model. It can be used for both covering a cake as a base coat or for modelling.

This icing is extremely malleable and even when paper-thin will hold its shape beautifully. As the icing is white, it is easy to achieve true colours, both pastel and stronger colours. Like almond paste, food colourings can either be kneaded into the icing or painted on the finished item. To avoid colouring your hands at the same time, place the fondant icing and a few drops of colouring in a polythene bag before kneading. Fondant icing waiting to be modelled should be kept covered with a damp cloth or in an airtight container. The icing will dry quickly and cracking will occur if left exposed to the air.

Once moulded, the icing will dry in about 24 hours to a hard finish.

Rose

Illustrated in colour facing page 32

You will need:

yellow, orange or pink food colouring   kneaded fondant icing

Knead the food colouring, a few drops at a time, into the fondant until the desired colour. Mould a cone and press out the base to form a stand. Roll out the fondant on a surface lightly dusted with sifted icing sugar. Cut small circles with a plain cocktail cutter or the base of an icing nozzle. Press and mould each petal until fairly thin. Wrap a petal around the cone, turning the edges outwards. Repeat, overlapping each petal, until the rose is formed. When a number of roses are grouped together, colour some darker. These roses appear on the birthday cake on page 85.

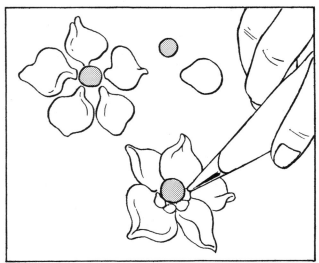

Christmas roses

Illustrated in colour facing page 32

You will need:

kneaded fondant icing   yellow food colouring
white royal icing   mimosa balls

Roll out the fondant on a surface dusted with sifted icing sugar. Cut small rounds with a plain cocktail cutter or the base of an icing nozzle. Mould each round into a petal shape and pinch the end to a point. Arrange five petals in an overlapping circle and secure in position with royal icing. Colour the remaining icing bright yellow and spoon into an icing bag fitted with a plain nozzle (No. 2). Place a mimosa ball in the centre of each flower. Pipe dots around the centre lifting the icing nozzle at the same time to form the stamens.

Daisy

Illustrated in colour facing page 32

You will need

kneaded fondant icing   pink or orange
yellow food colouring   food colouring

Colour a little of the fondant icing yellow for the centres. Colour the remainder pink, orange or leave white, roll out thinly and cut into small rectangles. Make a line of cuts or snips along one edge. Open out the fan shape. Roll pieces of the yellow fondant icing into small balls then pinch out and mould a stalk. Wrap a fan shape piece of fondant icing around each centre. Pinch the end of each petal to a point.

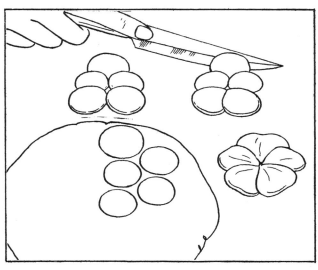

Pansy

You will need:

kneaded fondant icing mauve food colouring
yellow food colouring   brown food colouring

Divide the fondant in half and colour yellow and mauve. Roll out thinly. Using a plain cocktail cutter or the base of an icing nozzle, cut five petals for each flower. Place a petal in the palm of the hand, press with the thumb to flatten and lift the outside edge. Make one petal a little larger than the other four. Arrange the petals with the larger petal at the top and the four smaller petals grouped underneath. Mark in the petal lines with a pointed knife. Carefully paint in the details with the brown food colouring.

Leaves

Illustrated in colour facing page 32

You will need:

green food colouring   blue food colouring
kneaded fondant icing

Knead a few drops of green food colouring into the fondant until an even colour. Roll out on a surface lightly dusted with sifted icing sugar. Cut into leaf shapes with a small pointed knife. Lift each leaf into the palm of the hand and mould each end into a point. Stir a drop of blue colouring into a little green colouring to make a slightly darker green colour. Using a fine paint brush, mark in the veins on each leaf. Alternatively, mark in the veins with a pointed knife or skewer.
Note The same technique can be used to make leaves from almond paste.

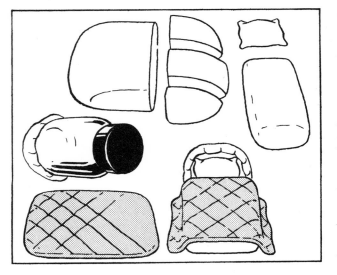

Baby's cradle

You will need:

about 100 g (4 oz) kneaded fondant icing	blue or pink food colouring white glacé icing

Divide the fondant icing in half and mould one piece into a roll 7·5 cm (3 in) long and 2·5 cm (1 in) in diameter. Flatten one side for the cradle base. Divide the remaining piece into three and knead pink or blue colouring into one piece. Roll out the coloured piece, cut into a rectangle and mark into diamonds with a knife for the quilt. Place over the cradle base. Shape one piece of white fondant to make the pillow. Roll out the remaining fondant into a rectangle for the hood and place over a small jar until set in shape. Assemble the cradle.

Mouse and bottle

Illustrated in colour facing page 32

You will need:

about 150 g (5 oz) kneaded fondant icing	pink food colouring cocoa powder nylon bristles

Shape half the fondant into a baby's bottle, flatten the base. Colour a little fondant pink and shape the bottle teat. Knead sieved cocoa powder into most of the remaining fondant. Roll two balls, one larger than the other, for the body and head. Roll four ropes for the arms and legs. Shape the feet, hands and tail. Roll small balls for the eyes and nose. Stick the bristles into the face. Shape two ears. Mould a pink night cap, feet pads and inner ears and position. Assemble the pieces.

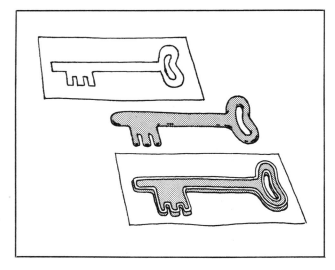

Key

You will need:

food colouring kneaded fondant icing	royal icing

Draw a key shape on a piece of greaseproof paper. Cut out and use as a pattern. Knead the chosen colouring into the fondant icing. Roll out the fondant icing 0·25 cm ($\frac{1}{8}$ in) thick on a surface dusted with sifted icing sugar. Place the pattern on the icing and carefully cut around the shape with a pointed knife. Leave until completely dry. Colour the royal icing either the same as the fondant or a contrasting colour. Spoon into an icing bag fitted with a plain nozzle (No. 2). Pipe a line around the outside edge of the key to give a bolder outline.

Crystallising flowers and leaves

Illustrated in colour facing page 32

Flowers, petals and leaves crystallised at home usually look more attractive than the commercially prepared ones and are quite easy to make. Once crystallised, they can be stored in an airtight container in a cool dry place and used as an attractive decoration on all kinds of cakes.

You can crystallise most flowers, except those grown from bulbs as they are poisonous. You will get the best results from flattish flowers with a small number of petals, e.g. violets, primroses, rose petals, fruit blossoms — apple, pear or cherry. Choose whole flowers that are fresh and free from damage, bruises or brown marks. Pick them in the morning once the dew has lifted and the petals are completely dry.

Leaves can also be crystallised — mint are probably the most popular because of their pleasant taste. Be just as selective when picking the leaves, making sure they are blemish free.

There are two methods of crystallising. For the simpler method, the flowers or leaves are painted with egg white and sprinkled with caster sugar. These can be kept for 1–2 months only. For the second method, the flowers are painted with gum arabic, left to absorb it and then coated with caster sugar. These flowers will store well for many months in a screw top jar.

Crystallised leaves
(Method 1)

You will need:
1 egg white   caster sugar
leaves

Whisk the egg white lightly. Divide the leaves, leaving a short piece of stalk if possible. Paint both sides of the leaf with egg white and then sprinkle both sides with caster sugar. Shake off surplus sugar and leave to dry. If necessary, sprinkle a second time with sugar to ensure the leaves are evenly coated. Leave to dry completely before storing in a screw top jar.

Crystallised flowers and petals (Method 2)

You will need:
15 g (½ oz)   caster sugar
  gum arabic   flowers or petals
30 ml (2 tbsp)
  rose water

Place the gum arabic and rose water in a small screw top jar. Shake together for 2–3 minutes. Leave for 1–3 hours until the gum arabic has dissolved. Paint both sides of the petals with this mixture. Place on a wire rack or waxed paper and leave for about 24 hours until the solution has been absorbed. Sprinkle both sides of the petals with caster sugar and shake off the surplus. Sprinkle with sugar a second time until evenly coated and then leave to dry.

Chocolate decorations

Illustrated in colour facing page 32

Cooking chocolate, plain or milk, can be used for cake decorations but for special occasions and good results use the chocolate cake covering (not cooking chocolate).

Break the chocolate into small pieces. Place in a double boiler, small basin or on a plate and stand over a pan of hot, not boiling, water. Leave the chocolate until it has completely melted.

It is important not to overheat the chocolate or let the water boil as the smallest drop of water or condensation in the chocolate will spoil it.

When making chocolate shapes, leaves or squares, leave the chocolate to set in a cool place. Do not dry in the refrigerator as the chocolate will set with a dull finish.

Leave any surplus chocolate to set completely. It can then be lifted easily from the paper, bowl or utensil and stored in a screw top jar or airtight container. Remelt and use it again.

All chocolate shapes can be stored for several weeks in an airtight container in a cool place or the refrigerator.

Chocolate shapes

Spread the melted chocolate in a thin even layer on a piece of non-stick or waxed paper and leave until almost set.

Use a small plain, fluted or shaped pastry cutter or cocktail cutters to make the shapes. Place the cutter on the chocolate and apply a firm but even pressure. Do not twist the cutter or the shape will be spoilt. Lift the cutter and continue cutting shapes in the chocolate. Leave the chocolate until firm and completely dry before carefully lifting the shapes with a round-bladed knife.

Chocolate curls

Spread the melted chocolate in a thick layer on a marble surface or non-stick or waxed paper and leave until completely set. Using a sharp knife held at an angle of 45°, push the knife across the chocolate scraping off a thin layer which will form a curl. Make sure your hands are cool when handling these curls as they will easily melt.

When you need a few chocolate curls in a hurry, 'peel' thin layers straight from the block of chocolate with a potato peeler or vegetable knife.

Chocolate rose leaves

The best time to pick rose leaves is in the morning, once the sun has had time to dry the dew. Pick fresh shiny leaves that are undamaged and with clearly marked veins. Wash them well and dry carefully on kitchen paper towel.

Using a round bladed knife or teaspoon, spread a thin but even layer of melted chocolate on the underside of each leaf, making sure the chocolate is spread right to the edges for a good shape. Alternatively, dip the leaves into the melted chocolate. Leave until set, chocolate side up, and completely dry. Carefully lift the tip of the rose leaf and peel back gently.

Chocolate squares and triangles

Spread the melted chocolate in a thin even layer on a piece of non-stick or waxed paper and leave until almost set.

For squares Mark into even sized squares with a sharp knife, using a ruler as a guide.

For triangles Mark diagonally across squares for even sided triangles. For long-sided triangles, mark the chocolate into rectangles and then mark in half.

Leave the chocolate until completely set and then carefully lift the shapes using a round-bladed knife.

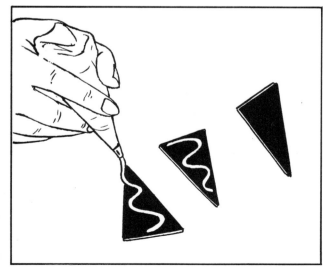

Piped chocolate shapes

Spread the melted chocolate in a thin even layer on a piece of non-stick or waxed paper and leave until almost set. Cut out the shapes as above.

Make up a greaseproof icing bag but do not cut off the end. Fill with melted chocolate, plain or milk as a contrast, and then snip off the tip. Pipe the chocolate over the shapes in straight lines, loops or a zig-zag pattern. Leave until completely set before using.

Leave any surplus chocolate in the bag until it is set. The bag can then be peeled away and chocolate stored in one piece for use again.

Christmas decorations

Illustrated in colour facing page 32

Christmas is always a busy time with plenty to do in the kitchen. It is nice to spend time decorating the Christmas cake but all too often it has to be done in a hurry. In this section we give you ideas for effective Christmas decorations, using either almond paste or royal icing. These decorations can either be made quickly and simply or made in advance and stored until needed.

Colour trimmings of almond paste green or red for holly or ivy leaves and holly berries, or colour and shape into a Santa Claus. There are two Santas; we have used the simpler version on the Christmas cake on page 100, complete with a sugar sleigh. Sparkling sugar bells always look attractive and are very quick and simple to make. If you have a little more time, run-out icing Christmas trees or holly leaves are well worth the effort for a more professional appearance.

There are other Christmas decorations in other sections of this chapter — see especially fondant Christmas roses on page 36.

Holly and ivy leaves

You will need:

almond paste   red food colouring
green food colouring

For holly leaves, colour the almond paste dark green by kneading a few drops of the colouring into almond paste. Roll out evenly on a piece of non-stick or waxed paper. Cut into small rectangles and then cut into a holly leaf shape using the base of an icing nozzle. Mark in the centre vein with a knife and leave until dry.

Colour some almond paste red and roll into small balls for berries.

For ivy leaves, colour the almond paste a lighter green and roll out as above. Cut out the leaf shape freehand and mark with veins then leave to dry.

Santa (1)

You will need:

50 g (2 oz) almond   stiff white royal or
  paste   glacé icing
red food colouring   blue glacé icing
orange food colouring   (optional)
cocktail stick

Colour two-thirds of the almond paste red and shape into the body and hat. Mark the arms on the body with a knife and hollow out the hat to fit the head. Colour the remaining almond paste orange, roll into a ball and insert the cocktail stick. Using an icing bag fitted with a plain nozzle (No. 2) and white icing, pipe in the arms, beard, eyes, nose and hat bobble. Pipe in blue eyes if wished. Leave the pieces to dry before assembling. This Santa decorates the Christmas cake on page 100.

Santa (2)

You will need:

about 175 g (6 oz) almond paste
red food colouring
pink food colouring
white royal icing
silver balls

Colour almost half the almond paste red. Divide the red almond paste and use 35 g (1¼ oz) to make the body, 15 g (½ oz) for each arm and the hat. Divide the uncoloured almond paste and use 40 g (1½ oz) to make the lower body and legs; 7 g (¾ oz) for the two hands; 15 g (½ oz) for the head. Colour this pink. The remainder is for the moustache and beard. Mould the legs into a sitting position. Fit the body over the legs. Mould tiny balls of red for the nose and mouth. Assemble Santa and, using a plain nozzle, pipe icing around the cuffs, coat, hat and other features.

Sugar bells

You will need:

50 g (2 oz) caster sugar
egg white
white royal or glacé icing
silver balls

For a sugar bell mould, use a plastic or metal Christmas bell decoration with the clapper removed. Place the sugar in a bowl with just enough egg white to moisten the sugar. Spoon the mixture into the mould, push down well and then turn out; tap gently on the rim if necessary. Leave until the outside of the bell is dry enough to handle and the centre still soft. Carefully scoop out the centre with a cocktail stick or small knife and reuse to make more bells. Pipe a little icing into each bell and top with a silver ball for a clapper.

Sugar bells appear on the cake on page 97.

Run-out Christmas trees

Used for decoration on the Christmas cake on page 98.

You will need:

white royal icing
green royal icing

Draw the outline of the Christmas tree on a piece of non-stick or waxed paper. Draw a vertical line down the centre of each tree. Using an icing bag fitted with a plain nozzle (No. 2) and white icing, pipe around the outline of half of each tree. Using an icing bag fitted with a plain nozzle (No. 2) and green icing, pipe around the outline of the other half then pipe a vertical line down the centre of each tree. Flood one half of the tree with white icing and the other half with green icing. Leave for about 24 hours until completely dry before carefully peeling off the paper.

Modelling with almond paste

Almond paste is perhaps one of the easiest modelling materials. Great care should be taken not to over-knead it as this makes the almond paste oily and difficult to handle. The addition of a little icing sugar can sometimes revert the paste to the right consistency. For cut-out shapes, roll out almond paste either on a surface dusted with sifted icing sugar or between two sheets of non-stick or waxed paper.

For fruits, animals and figures it is best to colour the almond paste before modelling. This is done by kneading food colouring into the almond paste a little at a time until the correct colour is achieved. To prevent colouring your hands at the same time, place the almond paste and the colouring in a polythene bag before kneading. When making flowers, roses in particular, divide the almond paste and add varying amounts of colouring to the different pieces. The rose can then be modelled with a realistic darker centre and paler outside petals.

A very effective finish can be obtained by painting diluted food colouring on to the modelled piece with a fine paint brush. A more subtle colouring can be achieved in this way.

Note Almond paste will dry out quickly so always keep it covered with a damp cloth, or place in an airtight container or polythene bag.

Violet

You will need:

violet food colouring	almond paste violet balls

Knead a few drops of food colouring into the almond paste until the desired colour. Roll out the almond paste thinly on a surface lightly dusted with sifted icing sugar. Cut four small oval petals for each flower and one large oval petal. Mould each petal to round the edges and gently shape them. Assemble the flower with the four petals together and the larger petal at the bottom. Push gently but firmly together. Place one ball in the centre of each violet.

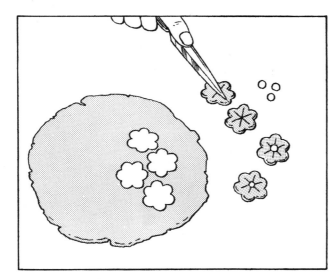

Primula

You will need:

yellow or pink food colouring	almond paste

Colour the almond paste or leave the natural colour. Roll out either on a surface lightly dusted with sifted icing sugar or between pieces of non-stick paper. Using a small fluted cocktail cutter, cut out the flowers. Lift carefully to prevent mis-shaping the petals. Mark in the petal lines with a fine skewer or a pointed knife. Knead a little colouring into the trimmings until a darker colour than the petals. Roll into small balls and place one in the centre of each primula. Use the flowers singly or place in small overlapping clusters.

These flowers have been used to decorate the Simnel cake on page 103.

Dahlia

You will need:

pink or yellow food colouring	almond paste white glacé icing

Knead a little colouring into the almond paste and roll out thinly. Cut five small triangles for the petals of each flower. Mould the three corners until slightly rounded and make a small slit down the centre of each petal. Mark the centre line from the slit to the petal base. Mould small balls of almond paste and flatten slightly. Place one petal on top and press gently. Place the remaining petals in an overlapping circle. Using a plain nozzle (No. 2) and glacé icing, pipe a dot in the centre of each flower. Pipe a circle of smaller dots around the centre one.

Strawberry, grapes, bananas

Illustrated in colour facing page 32

You will need:

almond paste	cloves
red food colouring	brown food colouring
green food colouring	small paper cases

Strawberry Colour some almond paste red and shape into a rounded cone. Roll over the medium surface of a grater. Colour a little almond paste green for the hull and assemble.
Bunch of grapes Colour some almond paste pale green, shape into a cone and flatten. Roll small balls for grapes and place on the cone.
Bananas Shape the bananas and paint with some brown colouring. Stick in a clove 'stalk'.

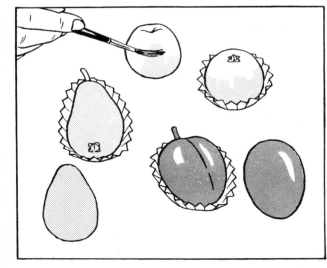

Pear, apple, plum

Illustrated in colour facing page 32

You will need:

almond paste	pink food colouring
green food colouring	blue food colouring
cloves	small paper cases

Pear Colour some paste pale green, roll into a cone and mould into a plump pear shape. Press a clove into the base and top. Paint a little pink colouring on one side.
Apple Colour some paste pale green and roll into a ball. Press a clove into the top and bottom. Paint pink colouring on one side.
Plum Colour some paste purple with pink and blue colouring. Roll into a rounded oval. Mark a line down one side. Press a clove into the top. Place each fruit in a paper case.

Orange, lemon and pineapple

Illustrated in colour facing page 32

You will need:

almond paste	cloves
orange food colouring	green food colouring
yellow food colouring	small paper cases

Orange Colour almond paste orange and roll into balls. Mark oranges into segments, if liked.
Lemon Colour some almond paste yellow and mould into a plump oval. Roll over the fine surface of a grater. Press in a clove at one end.
Pineapple Colour some almond paste yellow and roll into a plump oval. Mark a criss-cross pattern. Colour some almond paste green. Shape a small rectangle and snip along one edge. Roll up for pineapple top.

Place each fruit in a small paper case.

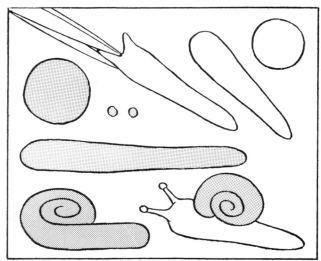

Snail

You will need:

about 50 g (2 oz)	cocoa powder
almond paste	

Divide the almond paste into two pieces and knead sifted cocoa powder into one half. Roll some plain almond paste into a ball. Roll into a rope, one end thicker than the other for the body. Make two cuts with a pair of scissors in the thick end and mould into two feelers. Roll a piece of chocolate almond paste into a rope. Roll the chocolate rope into a coil for the shell. Place the chocolate shell on top of the body. Roll two tiny pieces of chocolate almond paste into balls and top the feelers for eyes.

Chocolate rabbit

Illustrated in colour facing page 32

You will need:

about 50 g (2 oz)	cocoa powder
almond paste	

Leave a small piece of almond paste uncoloured. Knead sifted cocoa powder into the remaining paste. Roll about half of the chocolate almond paste into a ball. Shape into a plump cone and cut the pointed end in half. Open out for the paws. Roll a smaller piece into a ball for the head. Shape into a cone and cut the pointed end in half. Shape into ears. Place the head on top of the body. Roll the uncoloured paste into a ball for the tail and two smaller balls for eyes. Place in position. Roll two tiny pieces of chocolate into balls and place on top of eyes.

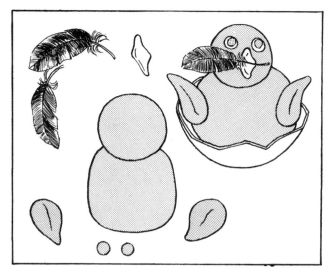

Easter chick

You will need:

about 50 g (2 oz) almond paste
orange food colouring

white glacé icing
clean egg shell
small feather

Roll most of the almond paste into two balls, one larger than the other. Place one ball on top of the other. Roll two small flattened cones for wings. Mark a line down the centre of each wing with a knife. Place in position on the body. Colour a little paste orange and shape into a diamond for the beak. Fold almost in half and place in position. Pipe two dots of icing for the eyes and top each with a small ball of almond paste. Place the chick in the shell with a feather in its beak.

The Easter chick appears on the Simnel cake on page 103.

Boy

Illustrated in colour facing page 32

You will need:

about 50 g (2 oz) almond paste
cocktail sticks

red food colouring
blue food colouring

Shape about a third of uncoloured almond paste into a rectangle. Snip into the centre and open out for the trousers. Push a cocktail stick down each leg. Shape the feet and position. Shape an oval for the body. Roll a thick rope for both arms and place on top of the body. Push a cocktail stick through the centre of the body. Roll a ball for the head and shape a smaller ball into a cap. Roll small balls for the eyes and buttons and shape a mouth. Assemble and paint with food colouring.

Girl

Illustrated in colour facing page 32

You will need:

about 50 g (2 oz) almond paste
cocktail sticks

green food colouring
red food colouring
blue food colouring

Shape about two-thirds of uncoloured almond paste into a wedge. Squeeze in the centre for the waistline. Push a cocktail stick through the centre — top to bottom and one widthways. Shape two feet and stick to the bottom of the skirt. Shape two half circles for the sleeves. Roll two ropes for the arms and attach both to the body. Roll a small ball for the head. Shape two half circles and wrap around the head for hair. Roll small balls for the eyes and shape a mouth. Assemble the figure and paint with food colouring.

Decorating sponge and sandwich cakes

It is quick and simple to make and decorate a sponge or sandwich cake for a teatime treat or special occasion.

The cake is usually made from a Victoria sandwich mixture. For a lighter and more airy sponge use a genoese mixture or even a whisked sponge mixture, although this needs to be eaten on the day it is baked. Preparing a Victoria sandwich is made easier by using a soft tub margarine that requires less beating than block margarine or butter — the result is a light, airy and moist sponge. If you are in a hurry, try the one stage method for a sandwich cake (see page 121) — all the ingredients are simply beaten well together.

Baking sponge and sandwich cakes

A sandwich cake should be baked in the middle of the oven. It is best to place the two tins on separate shelves under one another and change them over half way through the cooking time. If the cakes are cooked side by side on the same shelf, the heat of the oven will rise between the two tins and cause the cakes to rise unevenly. Once cooked, leave the cakes to cool in the tin for about a minute before turning them out. Turn on to a wire rack and leave to cool completely before icing and decorating.

A sponge or sandwich cake is at its best if eaten on the same day it is cooked but the cakes, plain or decorated, can be stored successfully in an airtight container in a cool place for 3–4 days.

Don't be tempted to store the decorated cakes in the refrigerator as this will dry out the sponge very quickly. If the cake is decorated with chocolate shapes, the chocolate will lose its sheen and become dull.

When sandwiching the two cakes together (see page 23), select a complementary filling and covering. Chopped nuts, glacé fruits or chocolate chips can be stirred into butter cream if used for the filling.

Decorating the cakes

The decorated cakes in this section range from a simple but effective feather-iced cake to the more complex designs using chocolate shapes made in the Hand-made decorations section (see pages 36–47).

Glacé icing used for these cakes should be quite stiff; to test, make sure the icing will coat the back of a spoon. The consistency of the icing can easily be altered by adding a little more sifted icing sugar to thicken or a little more water to thin it slightly.

The consistency of *butter cream* can also be changed by altering the balance of ingredients slightly. Add more sifted icing sugar for a thicker icing or a little fruit juice or coffee essence etc. to thin it. When spreading the sides and top of the cake with butter cream the icing should be quite soft and fluffy. For piping a decoration, the butter cream should be a little stiffer.

Coating the cake sides

To decorate the side of the round sandwich cake, a simple effect can be achieved by spreading the sides with jam or butter cream and coating with chopped nuts, coconut or chocolate vermicelli. The simplest way to do this is to spread the coating on a piece of greaseproof paper. Spread the sides of the sandwiched cakes with jam or butter cream and then slide the cake to the edge of the working surface. Carefully slide the cake on to the palm of one hand. Place the other on top and turn the cake on its side. Now you are ready to roll the sides of the cake in the coating. Cover about half the cake, then shake the greaseproof paper gently and all the remaining coating will return to the centre of the paper. Continue rolling the cake to cover the rest of the side.

Baking different shapes

For a change from the round cake, make and decorate a Swiss roll or bake the basic Victoria sandwich mixture in a shaped tin — a loaf tin or ring mould. Use the guide on page 104 if you decide to use a different shaped cake tin such as a heart. Pages 57 to 60 show some ideas for decorating these cakes or for a festive Yule log.

Feather iced cakes (*page 63*), Iced fancies
(*page 64*), Chocolate hedgehogs (*page 68*),
Chocolate boxes (*page 65*), Marzipan flower cakes
(*page 62*), Mushroom meringues (*page 66*)

Feather iced sandwich cake

You will need:
two 20·5-cm (8-in) round Victoria sandwich cakes
raspberry or strawberry jam
white glacé icing using 225 g (8 oz) icing
    sugar etc.
pink food colouring

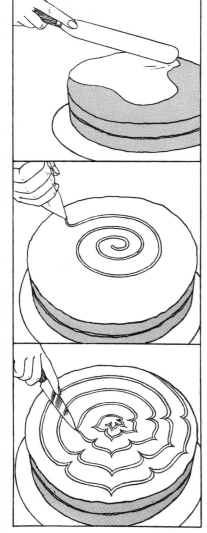

Sandwich the cakes together with the jam. Place 30 ml (2 tbsp) glacé icing in a small bowl and stir in the pink colouring to give a deep colour. Spoon into a greaseproof icing bag without a nozzle. Pour the white icing on to the top of the cake and spread almost to the edges with a round-bladed knife. It will then flow to the edge without dripping over.

Work quickly, so the white icing does not form a skin. Snip the tip from the greaseproof icing bag. Pipe a continuous circular line starting in the centre of the cake and work towards the outside edge.

Using a skewer or pointed knife, *quickly* draw it from the centre to the outside edge of the cake in a straight line. Leave a space of about 2·5 cm (1 in) then draw a line from the outside edge towards the centre to complete the feather or webb pattern. Repeat the pattern around the top of the cake then leave to set.

Basket birthday cake (*page 84*), Rosebud cake (*page 83*)

Split top sandwich cake

You will need:
two 20·5-cm (8-in) round Victoria sandwich cakes
almond butter cream using 225 g (8 oz) icing
    sugar etc.
175 g (6 oz) raspberry or strawberry jam
icing sugar

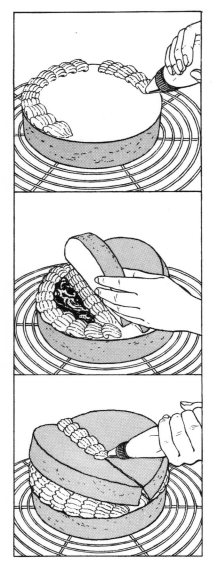

Leave one cake whole and cut the other in half. Spoon the butter cream into an icing bag fitted with an eight point star nozzle. Pipe a shell border around the top edge of the base cake leaving two 2·5-cm (1-in) spaces opposite each other.

Place the jam in a saucepan and heat gently until a pouring consistency; leave to cool. Spoon the jam on to the base of the cake and spread it to the piped border. Pipe two shell borders on top of the jam in each half of the cake to meet the shell borders around the top edge. Place the cake halves in position, allowing the butter cream to support their weight.

Dust the top of the cake with sifted icing sugar. Pipe a shell border along the join of the split top.

Note This design can be used when filling a sandwich cake with fresh cream and pieces of fresh or canned fruits.

Daisy chain sandwich cake

You will need:
two 20·5-cm (8-in) round Victoria sandwich cakes
lemon curd
white glacé icing using 175 g (6 oz) icing sugar etc.
yellow food colouring
green food colouring

Decoration
5 mimosa balls

Sandwich the cakes together with lemon curd. Make a greaseproof paper collar to stand 2·5 cm (1 in) above the top of the cake. Wrap it around the cake tightly and secure with a paper clip. Reserve 60 ml (4 tbsp) white glacé icing and colour the remainder yellow. Spoon the yellow icing on top of the cake, spread just to the edges and leave to set for about 1 hour.

Note A greaseproof paper collar is not needed if a thin layer of icing is preferred.

Place half the reserved icing in an icing bag fitted with a plain nozzle (No. 2). Colour the remainder a pale green and spoon into a greaseproof icing bag without a nozzle. Place the mimosa balls in position on the top of the cake and pipe the outline of six petals in white icing around each.

Snip the end off the greaseproof icing bag filled with green icing and pipe looped stems between the flowers. Cut the tip of the bag again into a neat point and pipe five pointed leaves between the flowers (see pages 30–31). Leave to set.

Chocolate triangle cake

You will need:
two 20·5-cm (8-in) round chocolate or coffee
    Victoria sandwich cakes
coffee or chocolate butter cream using 100 g
    (4 oz) icing sugar etc.
chocolate glacé icing using 225 g (8 oz) icing
    sugar etc.
icing sugar

Decoration
6 or 7 chocolate triangles (see page 41)

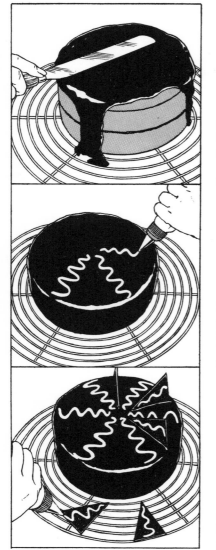

Sandwich the cakes together with the butter cream. Place the cake on a wire rack with a large plate underneath to catch any surplus icing. Reserve 45 ml (3 tbsp) glacé icing. Pour the remainder over the cake and spread over the top and side, making sure the cake is completely covered.

Stir enough sifted icing sugar into the reserved chocolate glacé icing to make a paler icing of a stiffer consistency. Spoon into an icing bag fitted with a plain nozzle (No. 2). Pipe six or seven graduated zig-zag lines from the centre of the cake to the outer edge.

Using the same icing bag, pipe a graduated zig-zag line on each of the chocolate triangles. When the icing on the cake is set but not completely dry, place the chocolate triangles in an upright position.

Orange and coconut sandwich cake

Illustrated in colour facing page 33

You will need:
two 20·5-cm (8-in) round Victoria sandwich cakes
apricot jam
toasted desiccated coconut
white glacé icing using 175 g (6 oz) icing
    sugar etc.
orange food colouring

Decoration
small crystallised orange segments

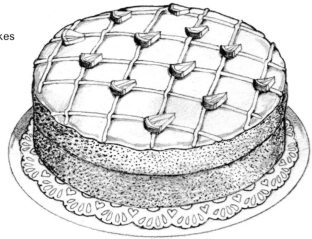

Sandwich the cakes together with apricot jam. Place 60 ml (4 tbsp) apricot jam in a saucepan and heat gently. Sieve the jam and while still warm brush over the side of the cake. Spread the coconut on a sheet of greaseproof paper. Turn the cake on its side, hold firmly between both hands and roll in the coconut until evenly coated.

Colour the glacé icing a pale orange. Reserve 45 ml (3 tbsp) icing and colour this a deeper orange. Spoon the pale orange icing on top of the cake and spread almost to the edges — it will then flow to the edge without dripping over. Leave to set. Spoon the darker orange icing into an icing bag fitted with a plain nozzle (No. 2). Pipe five or six evenly spaced straight lines across the top of the cake.

Turn the cake and pipe five or six evenly spaced straight lines across the first lines to form diamonds. Cut the orange segments in half and place in a pattern on top of the cake. Leave to set.

Orange and praline sandwich cake

You will need:
two 20·5-cm (8-in) round Victoria sandwich cakes
apricot jam
orange butter cream using 225 g (8 oz) icing
    sugar etc.
white praline using 40 g (1½ oz) granulated
    sugar etc. (see page 14)

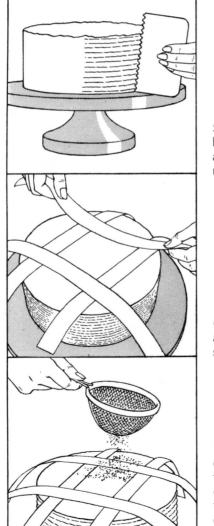

Sandwich the cakes together with the apricot jam. Spread half the butter cream over the top and side of the cake. Draw a serrated icing comb around the side of the cake to give a ribbed effect.

Cut four strips of greaseproof paper about 2 cm (¾ in) wide and 30·5 cm (12 in) long. Arrange the greaseproof paper strips on top of the cake in a crossways pattern.

Place the white praline in a sieve and shake gently over the cake until the top is covered thickly but evenly in praline. Lift the strips of greaseproof paper gently, taking care not to disturb the praline. Place the cake on a serving plate. Spoon the remaining butter cream into an icing bag fitted with an eight point star nozzle. Pipe a shell border around the top and base edges.

Coffee and walnut sandwich cake

Illustrated in colour facing page 33

You will need:
two 20·5-cm (8-in) round Victoria sandwich cakes
coffee butter cream using 225 g (8 oz) icing
    sugar etc.

Decoration
50 g (2 oz) walnuts, chopped
7 whole walnuts

Sandwich the cakes together with about a fifth of the butter cream. Cover the side of the cake thinly with butter cream. Spread the chopped walnuts over a piece of greaseproof paper. Turn the cake on its side and hold firmly between the palms of the hands. Roll the cake on the chopped walnuts until evenly coated.

Divide the remaining butter cream in half. Place half in an icing bag fitted with an eight point star nozzle. Spoon the remaining half on top of the cake. Using a round-bladed knife, spread the butter cream evenly over the surface to the top edge, then smooth with a paddling action.

Pipe a rope border along the top edge of the cake using the icing bag fitted with the star nozzle. Pipe the border moving the nozzle in a circular action, overlapping each loop. Place the whole walnuts in position.

Chocolate and mandarin cake

Illustrated in colour facing page 33

You will need:
two 20·5-cm (8-in) round Victoria chocolate
   sandwich cakes
chocolate butter cream using 225 g (8 oz) icing
   sugar etc.

Decoration
30 chocolate triangles (see page 41)
312-g (11-oz) can mandarin oranges, drained

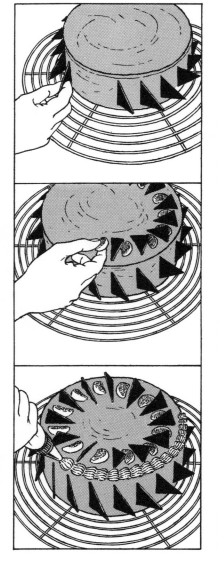

Sandwich the cakes together with about one fifth of the butter cream. Spoon a quarter of the remaining butter cream into an icing bag fitted with an eight point star nozzle. Spread the remaining butter cream over the top and side of the cake with a round-bladed knife. Place half the chocolate triangles around the side of the cake, tilted at an angle of 45°.

Arrange the remaining chocolate triangles in a pattern around the top edge of the cake with a mandarin orange segment between each. Tilt the chocolate triangles backwards at an angle of 45°.

Using the icing bag fitted with an eight point star nozzle, pipe a shell border around the top edge. Pipe a rosette in the centre of the cake and place a mandarin orange segment either side.

Ring cake

You will need:
butter cream using 225 g (8 oz) icing sugar etc.
yellow food colouring
1 quantity Victoria sandwich mixture baked in a
  1·4-litre (2½-pint) ring mould
round cake board (optional)

Decoration
almond paste primulas (see page 44)
almond paste leaves (see page 37)

Colour the butter cream a pale yellow and spoon half into an icing bag fitted with an eight point star nozzle. Spread the cake with the remaining butter cream, making sure the inside of the ring is also covered. Using a round-bladed knife, mark swirling patterns in the butter cream.

Carefully lift the cake on to the cake board or a round flat plate. Pipe a shell border around the bottom of the cake. Pipe an alternate shell border around the top edge of the cake, so one shell is on the top of the cake and the next on the side of the cake.

Arrange the flowers and leaves in a pattern on the cake. Push into the butter cream to secure.

Coffee and chocolate loaf

Illustrated in colour facing page 33

You will need:
1 quantity coffee Victoria sandwich mixture
   baked in a 450-g (1-lb) loaf tin
coffee glacé icing using 325 g (12 oz) icing
   sugar etc.
chocolate glacé icing using 100 g (4 oz) icing
   sugar etc.
rectangular cake board (optional)

Decoration
4 walnut halves

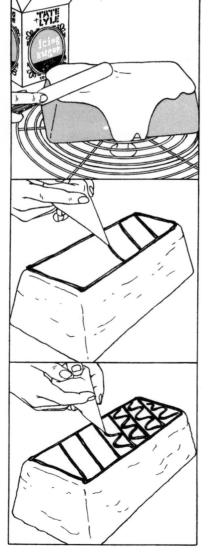

Place the cake on a wire rack with a large plate or tray underneath to catch the surplus icing. Spread the coffee glacé icing over the top and sides of the cake, making sure it is completely covered. Leave until completely set. Spoon the chocolate glacé icing into a greaseproof icing bag fitted with a plain nozzle (No. 2).

Pipe a straight line around the top edge of the cake using the chocolate glacé icing. Pipe even spaced straight lines diagonally across the top of the cake. Turn the icing bag nozzle up at the end of each line to make sure chocolate icing is not dripped on the cake.

Pipe zig-zag lines between the diagonal lines on the top of the cake. Pipe a little chocolate icing on the back of each walnut half and place in position. Leave to set.

Glacé fruit Swiss roll

You will need:
1 Swiss roll (see page 122)
50 g (2 oz) glacé fruits — cherries, angelica, pineapple
butter cream using 325 g (12 oz) icing sugar etc.
vanilla essence

Decoration
glacé pineapple and cherries
angelica leaves

Turn the cooked Swiss roll on to a wire rack and remove the lining paper. Trim all four edges neatly. Mark a line along one short side about 2·5 cm (1 in) from the edge. Place a clean sheet of greaseproof paper on the Swiss roll and roll up neatly with the seam underneath. Leave until completely cold. Chop the glacé fruits and stir into half the butter cream with the vanilla essence.

Carefully unroll the Swiss roll and remove the greaseproof paper. Spread the flavoured butter cream over the Swiss roll to within 1 cm ($\frac{1}{2}$ in) of the edge. Roll up the Swiss roll neatly with the seam underneath the cake.

Spoon the remaining butter cream into an icing bag fitted with an eight point star nozzle. Pipe straight lines along the length of the Swiss roll. Pipe two rows of shell border down the centre of the top of the cake. Pipe even spaced rosettes in between the shell borders. Place glacé fruits and angelica leaves between the rosettes.

Yule log

You will need:
1 chocolate Swiss roll (see page 123)
50 g (2 oz) seedless raisins
15 ml (1 tbsp) brandy
chocolate butter cream using 325 g (12 oz)
    icing sugar etc.
icing sugar
cake board (optional)

Decoration
almond paste holly leaves and berries (see
    page 42)

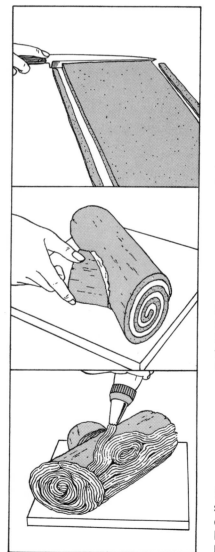

Turn the cooked Swiss roll on to a wire rack and remove the lining paper. Trim all four edges neatly. Mark a line along one short side about 2·5 cm (1 in) from the edge. Place a clean sheet of greaseproof paper on the Swiss roll and roll up neatly with the seam underneath. Leave until cold. Stir the raisins and brandy into a third of the butter cream. Unroll the Swiss roll, spread with butter cream and roll up.

Cut a thick diagonal slice from one end of the Swiss roll. Spread the diagonal end with butter cream and secure to the Swiss roll about half way along the side. Place the log on the cake board if used. Spoon the remaining butter cream into an icing bag fitted with an eight point star nozzle.

Pipe lines of butter cream over the log. Pipe in one or two swirls of icing to represent knots in the wood. Pipe butter cream over the three ends of the log. Dredge the whole cake lightly with sifted icing sugar. Place the holly leaves and berries in place for decoration.

Decorating small cakes

A selection of decorated small or individual cakes always look pretty at tea time, whether a simple afternoon tea or as part of a children's party spread. Many little cakes can be made from a basic fairy cake mixture. They are best baked in small batches and eaten on the same day as they tend to dry out during storage, however carefully you pack them.

Baking small cakes
The mixture can either be baked in greased patty tins or spooned into paper cases before baking. These are best placed inside patty tins to support the paper cases and the mixture during cooking, giving more even-shaped cakes.

Freezing small cakes
They can of course be frozen — open freeze un-iced fairy cakes and then pack into polythene bags and seal. Pack cut sponge shapes e.g. cubes for chocolate boxes, with a piece of waxed paper between each, into a polythene container and seal. Defrost completely before icing and decorating the cakes.

Icing and decorating small cakes
For good results when icing fairy cakes they need to have a reasonably flat top. If they rise to a peak during cooking, allow to cool completely and then carefully trim away the top with a sharp knife. Brush away any surplus crumbs from the top of the cakes — the crumbs may mix in with the icing and spoil the finished results.

They may be simply decorated by icing with a coat of glacé icing and then topping with half a glacé cherry and angelica leaves; chocolate buttons; small pieces of crystallised fruit, or sprinkling with grated chocolate or desiccated coconut with a little food colouring stirred in to give a pale colour. Keep a selection of cake decorations — tiny sweets, crystallised flowers, chocolate buttons — in airtight containers to decorate cakes with the minimum of fuss.

A similar sponge base is used for the Iced fancies, but the mixture is baked in a square tin and then cut into shapes. Never waste the trimmings, they can be used for trifles. When icing the fancies, make the glacé icing fairly stiff. For special occasions or a really smooth finish, the cakes can be covered with a thin layer of almond paste held in place with a little apricot glaze.

When piping a glacé icing decoration on little cakes, such as Funny faces, it is sometimes quicker and simpler to use a greaseproof icing bag with just the tip carefully snipped off — no need for a nozzle. Good results can be achieved because the piping is completed quickly and the icing does not have time to penetrate the greaseproof paper or ruin the tip of the bag.

Fairy cakes

100 g (4 oz) butter or margarine
100 g (4 oz) caster sugar
2 eggs, beaten
100 g (4 oz) self raising flour

Place 12–16 paper cases on baking sheets, or for a better final shape put them into patty tins. Cream the butter or margarine and sugar until pale and fluffy. Add the egg a little at a time, beating well after each addition. Fold in the flour using a tablespoon. Two-thirds fill the cases with the mixture and bake in the oven at 190°C (375°F) mark 5 for 15–20 minutes until golden.
Makes 12–16 cakes

VARIATIONS
Fold in one of the following:

50 g (2 oz) dates, chopped
50 g (2 oz) glacé cherries, chopped
50 g (2 oz) chocolate chips
50 g (2 oz) crystallised ginger, chopped

Marzipan flower cakes

Illustrated in colour facing page 48 and on the jacket

You will need:
12 fairy cakes baked in pink paper cases
white glacé icing using 225 g (8 oz) icing
    sugar etc.
100 g (4 oz) almond paste
pink food colouring
green food colouring
icing sugar

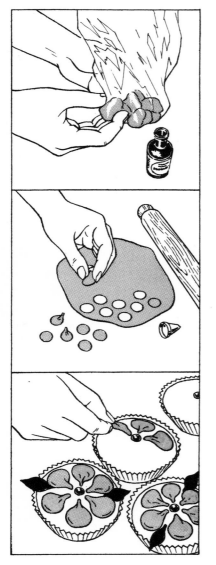

The top of the cakes needs to be fairly flat. If they have risen, trim away the peak. Place the cakes on a flat surface and spoon icing on each cake, using just enough to cover the top. Spread the icing to the edge of each cake and leave to set. Colour two-thirds of the almond paste pink and one-third a pale green by kneading the colouring into the almond paste.

Roll out the pink and the green almond paste on a surface lightly dusted with sifted icing sugar. Cut 72 petals from the pink almond paste with the base of an icing nozzle. Pinch one side of each to shape the petal. Knead the surplus pink almond paste and divide into 12 pieces. Roll each into a small ball. Make 24 leaf shapes by cutting the green almond paste into 0·5-cm (¼-in) strips and then into diamond-shaped pieces. Shape the sides of the leaves and then mark the veins on the leaves with a pointed knife.

Arrange six petals in an even spaced circle on the top of each cake. Place one small ball of pink almond paste in the centre of each cake. Arrange two leaves, opposite each other on the top of each cake.

Feather iced cakes

Illustrated in colour facing page 48 and on the jacket

You will need:
12 fairy cakes baked in coloured paper cases
white glacé icing using 225 g (8 oz) icing
    sugar etc.
cocoa powder
pink food colouring

The tops of the cakes need to be fairly flat. If they have risen, trim away the peak. Place the cakes on a flat surface. Divide the icing into three — colour one portion chocolate, one portion pink and leave one white. Cover four cakes each in pink, chocolate and white icing. Spoon icing on each cake, just enough to cover the top. Spread the icing to the edge of each cake with a round-bladed knife.

Spoon the remaining icings into separate greaseproof icing bags and snip off the tip. Working quickly so the icing does not set, pipe parallel lines 0·5 cm (¼ in) apart or circles on the top of the cakes in a contrasting colour.

Draw a skewer or pointed knife through the piped icing in one direction and then in the opposite direction to make the feather pattern. *Work quickly* or the icing will form a skin and set before the pattern has been formed.

Iced fancies

Illustrated in colour facing page 48

You will need:
1 quantity vanilla Victoria sandwich mixture
white glacé icing using 325 g (12 oz) icing
    sugar etc.
pink and yellow food colouring
paper cases
cocoa powder

Decoration
mimosa balls
crystallised violets
grated chocolate

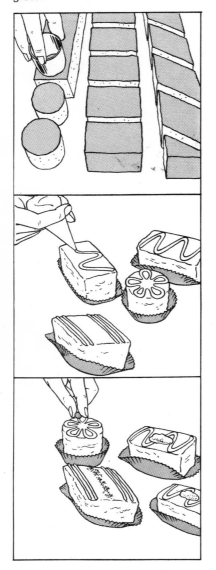

Turn the Victoria sandwich mixture into a greased and lined 18×23·5-cm (7×10-in) rectangular cake tin. Bake in the oven at 190°C (375°F) mark 5 for about 25 minutes, until well risen and golden brown. Turn out on to a wire rack and leave until cold. Cut the cake into three strips. Cut four circles from one piece, five rectangles from another and four diamonds from the last piece of cake. Place the cakes on a wire rack with a plate or tray underneath to collect surplus icing. Divide the glacé icing into four. Colour one portion pink, one yellow and leave a double portion white.

Using about two thirds of the white icing, coat the top and sides of the diamond-shaped cakes. Coat the top and sides of the circular cakes yellow and the rectangular ones pink. Leave until set. Place each cake in a paper case. Divide the remaining white icing and stir sifted cocoa into one third. Spoon both the chocolate and white icing into separate greaseproof icing bags fitted with plain nozzles (No. 2). Pipe a zig-zag line in white icing on the rectangular cakes and the outline of petals on the circular cakes. Pipe straight lines in chocolate icing on the diamond-shaped cakes.

Leave the piped icing until almost set before adding the decorations. Place a mimosa ball in the centre of each flower on the circular cakes. Place a crystallised violet in the centre of each rectangular cake. Carefully sprinkle grated chocolate on to the diamond-shaped cakes between the piped lines with the aid of a palette knife. *Makes 13 cakes*

Apricot mother birthday cake (*page 85*)

Chocolate boxes

Illustrated in colour facing page 48

You will need:
1 quantity chocolate Victoria sandwich mixture
vanilla butter cream using 225 g (8 oz) icing
    sugar etc.
chocolate squares (see page 41)
paper cases

Turn the chocolate Victoria sandwich mixture into a 19-cm (7½-in) square tin. Bake in the oven at 190°C (375°F) mark 5 for about 25 minutes until well risen. Turn out on to a wire rack and leave until cold. Cut the chocolate sponge into 3·5-cm (1½-in) strips. Cut each strip into 3·5-cm (1½-in) cubes.

Spread the four sides of each cake cube with a little butter cream. Place a square of chocolate on each side and gently push into the cake to secure.

Spoon the remaining butter cream into an icing bag fitted with an eight point star nozzle. Pipe a little butter cream on one side of the top of each cake as a hinge for the chocolate square lid. Pipe a neat shell border along the opposite side. Place a chocolate square on top, slightly wedged open by the shell border. Place each cake in a paper case. *Makes 25 cakes*

Golden anniversary cake (*page 93*),
Silver anniversary cake (*page 92*)

Mushroom meringues

Illustrated in colour facing page 48

You will need:

3 egg whites
175 g (6 oz) caster sugar
10 ml (2 tsp) coffee essence
chocolate butter cream using 225 g (8 oz) icing
    sugar etc.
paper cases

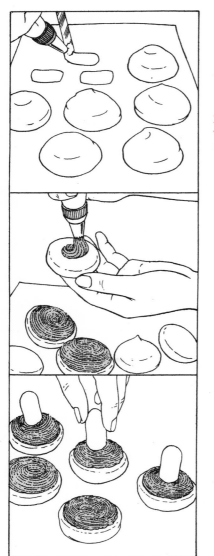

Whisk the egg whites very stiffly. Add half the sugar and whisk again until stiff and shiny. Fold in the remaining sugar and the coffee essence. Spoon the meringue mixture into an icing bag fitted with a large plain vegetable nozzle. Pipe 2·5–3·5-cm (1–1½-in) rounds on to a baking sheet covered with non-stick paper, for the mushroom heads. Pipe an equal number of stalks about 2·5–3·5 cm (1–1½ in) long. Cook in the oven at 110°C (225°F) mark ¼ for about 3 hours until the meringues are firm and crisp. Leave on a wire rack until completely cold.

Spoon the butter cream into an icing bag fitted with an eight point star nozzle. Pipe a large flat rosette on the flat side of each mushroom so the icing is almost to the edge.

Pipe a little butter cream on one end of each mushroom stalk. Place a stalk upright in the centre and push gently into the icing. Place the mushrooms in paper cases. *Makes about 18 cakes*

Note These are best eaten on the day they are made. The meringues can be stored without cream in an airtight tin until required.

Funny faces

You will need:
12 fairy cakes baked in coloured paper cases
white glacé icing using 225 g (8 oz) icing
    sugar etc.
pink and yellow food colouring
Smarties
cocoa powder
icing sugar

The tops of the cakes need to be fairly flat. If they have risen, trim away the peak. Place the cakes on a flat surface. Colour half the icing a pale apricot colour using a little pink and yellow colouring. Spoon icing on to each cake, using just enough to cover the top. Spread the icing to the edge of each cake with a round-bladed knife.

Place green, brown or lilac Smarties on the cakes for the eyes. Place red Smarties in position for the mouths. Divide the remaining icing into three. Colour one portion yellow, one portion pink and one portion chocolate. Each colour icing may need to be thickened by adding a little sifted icing sugar.

Spoon the icings into separate icing bags fitted with plain nozzles (No. 2) or make up greaseproof icing bags and snip off the tip. Using the coloured icings, pipe in the facial features, hair and bow ties.

Chocolate hedgehogs

Illustrated in colour facing page 48

You will need:
1 quantity chocolate Victoria sandwich mixture
chocolate butter cream using 225 g (8 oz) icing
    sugar etc.
whole cloves or currants
almond slivers
almond halves

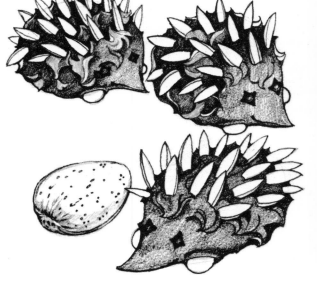

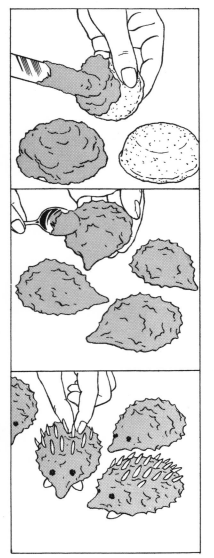

Divide the Victoria sandwich mixture between well greased round bottomed patty tins. Bake in the oven at 190°C (375°F) mark 5 for about 20 minutes until well risen. Turn out on to a wire rack and leave until cold. Turn each cake rounded side up and spread with butter cream.

Using a round-bladed knife or the back of a teaspoon, pull the butter cream into well formed peaks. Form a large peak for the hedgehog's nose. Stick two cloves into the icing just above the nose for the eyes.

Place all the almonds on a baking sheet and brown lightly in a hot oven or under the grill. Leave until cool. Stick the slivered almonds all over each hedgehog's back to represent the prickles. Place two almond halves under the hedgehog for feet and press gently into the cake. *Makes about 18 cakes*

Special occasion cakes

Everyone has birthdays and anniversaries, so everyone has the opportunity to celebrate with a beautifully iced cake. Once you have mastered the basics of cake decorating you will look for every excuse to show off your skills. This chapter includes cakes for everyone's special occasions: Christmas, birthdays, engagements, weddings, wedding anniversaries and christenings. Although each cake has been designed with an occasion in mind, many of the designs can be interchanged quite successfully, e.g. the pink christening cake on page 94 would make a beautiful birthday cake if the centre decorations were exchanged for pink and white fondant roses.

Throughout the chapter, excluding the wedding cakes, we have used similar sized cakes, about 23 cm (9 in), in most cases. If your celebration is very large you can, of course, use the same design on a larger cake. Turn to the chart on page 119 for a guide to the amount of cake mixture required to fill the size and shape of cake tin you have chosen and page 71 for a guide to the amount of almond paste and royal icing you will need to cover the cake.

Timing
Remember, each stage of cake icing takes time to dry so allow yourself plenty of time. The longer the cake is allowed to mature the better it will be — three months is about the best time but it will keep quite successfully much longer if well wrapped in foil and sealed and stored in a cool dry place. The addition of a little sherry or brandy at monthly intervals will also help to keep the cake moist. Pierce the surface of the cake with a fine skewer and pour over 30–45 ml (2–3 tbsp) sherry or brandy.

Allow about one week for the almond paste to dry out sufficiently before applying any icing.

It is easier to flat ice the side and the top of the cake separately, so allow 24 hours for either the side or top to dry before icing the other surface. Better results are usually achieved if a second thinner coat of icing is applied to the cake; if you plan to do this, allow 24–48 hours for the first coat to dry completely before applying the second coat.

Allow about 24 hours for the piped icing to dry out and make separate iced flowers, run-outs, etc. about 5–7 days before required.

Cake boards
An iced cake always looks better on a cake board, so select one at least 5 cm (2 in) larger than the cake to give plenty of room for a border to be piped around the base of the cake. The cake board can also be flat iced and decorated with piped icing (see the apricot cake on the jacket of the book), in which case you may prefer to have an even larger board.

Decorating with flowers
Until you become expert at piping flowers, you may prefer to use fabric flowers for decoration on the cake. Most department stores have a good selection either in the millinery or bridal department. Select sprays of flowers that can be separated easily to give a number of dainty flowers. You can also mix fabric flowers with a few hand-made flowers effectively — see the birthday cake on page 85.

Decorating with ribbons
While shopping for flowers, select suitable coloured ribbons or daintily embroidered borders from the haberdashery department. Use ribbons that contrast or tone with the colour of the cake. Thin ribbons can be tied with a little thread into neat rosettes, see the cake on page 93, or decorative parcel ribbon will stick to itself to make very pretty bows (see the cake on page 84).

Ribbons and lace have been used to make the **cradle** on the christening cake on page 95. Simply cover the base of a matchbox with pleated lace and secure with a little glue. Cut a piece from the slide-on cover 5 cm (1 in) wide, cover with a piece of satin ribbon and stick in place for the hood. Stick the two pieces together, place a coloured cotton wool ball inside and stick a small bow at the foot of the cradle.

Decorating Christmas cakes
For Christmas cakes you can make your own decorations (see pages 42–43) or, if you prefer, select small Christmas decorations like the fabric poinsettia used on the cake on page 99, or candles and ribbons (see the Christmas cake on page 96).

Wedding cakes

Planning the wedding cake

It is most important for the final overall result to choose the sizes of the tiers carefully, avoiding a combination that would look too heavy. Good proportions for a three-tier cake are 30·5, 23 and 15 cm (12, 9 and 6 in); for a two-tier cake 30·5 and 20·5 cm (12 and 8 in), 28 and 18 cm (11 and 7 in) or 25·5 and 15 cm (10 and 6 in). The bottom tier should be deeper than the upper ones, therefore cakes of 25·5–30·5 cm (10–12 in) diameter are generally made about 7·5 cm (3 in) deep, while those 18–23 cm (7–9 in) in diameter are 6·5 cm (2½ in) deep, and 12·5–15 cm (5–6 in) diameter cakes are 5 cm (2 in) deep. Don't attempt to make the larger sizes of cake unless you have an oven to cope with it, as you should allow at least 2·5 cm (1 in) space between the oven walls and the tin. For a three-tier cake, bake the two smaller cakes together and the largest one separately.

You can expect to cut 8–10 portions of cake from each 450 g (1 lb) cooked mixture. (See the chart on page 119.) So, if you have 20 guests and want to send out 20 'postings', you need 40 portions in all, meaning at least 2·3 kg (5 lb) of cake. If you wish to keep the top tier intact, the 2·3 kg (5 lb) must of course be additional to the top tier weight. When the reception is large, it is well worth making and icing an extra tier for behind-the-scenes cutting to expedite distribution among the guests.

Cake boards Silver is the usual colour (except for a golden wedding cake). The board should be 5 cm (2 in) larger than the cake, e.g. for a 20·5-cm (8-in) cake use a 25·5-cm (10-in) board. For a very large cake, use a board 10–12·5 cm (4–5 in) larger than the cake. You may also prefer to place a thin royal-iced board on the base cake to take the weight of the pillars and other two cakes; a piped decoration hides its edge. This should not be necessary if the base coats of icing have been hardened sufficiently.

Cake pillars Pillars between the base cake and the next tier are usually 9 cm (3½ in) high and those between the middle tier and top tier 7·5 cm (3 in) high. Cake pillars can be square or round for the respectively shaped cakes, or octagonal to use for either shape. All are available in white or silver coloured polythene or white plaster.

When to do what

2–3 months before Make the cake; when cold, prick at intervals with a fine skewer and spoon some brandy evenly over the surface. Wrap the cooked cakes in greaseproof paper and then in a double thickness of foil. Store for at least a month but preferably for 2–3 months in a cool dry place.

3–4 weeks before The baked cakes should have an even top but if not they can be levelled with a sharp knife. Apply the almond paste to each cake (see pages 17–18) and store loosely covered in a cool dry place for 1–2 weeks before applying the first coat of icing (see page 19).

10–14 days before Apply the first coat of royal icing and leave to dry for 1–2 days. Think about the design of the cake.

8–12 days before Apply the second coat of royal icing if necessary and leave to dry for 1–2 days. Make all separate or run-out decorations for the cake and leave to dry for 1–2 days.

Cutting a wedge Confectioners' wedding cakes sometimes have a pre-cut 'wedge' in the bottom tier to make the ceremonial cutting of the cake simpler. This is purely optional and is rarely done with home-made cakes, but for those who wish to do it, this is the method: Mark and cut a wedge from the bottom tier when the flat icing has dried, and prior to applying the decorative finish. The wedge should, of course, be cut so that it will fit back into the overall design of the cake. Tie the cut wedge with a good satin ribbon, protecting the ribbon with greaseproof paper on the sides of the wedge, and tie a neat bow on the outside. Replace the wedge and proceed with the decoration of the whole cake.

7 days before Plan the design well in advance. Make applied decorations at least two days before fixing them to the iced cake; preferably, complete all decorating a week before the wedding, but don't assemble the tiers until the very last possible time before the wedding.

When you have planned the cake design – the simplest can be very effective – draw the pattern on greaseproof paper the same size as the top of the cake. Then put the paper (template) on the top surface and prick out the key points on to the icing. Or use light pencil marks where the decoration is sure to cover them. Collect together the required number of 'applied' decorations like sugar flowers, run-out plaques or initials, and have ready-to-hand any bought decorations — silver leaves, heather, horseshoes, etc. — that you wish to add. It's a good idea, except for experienced cake decorators, to practise piped designs — lines, trellis, scrolls, borders — on a table surface or an upturned plate before actually piping them on to the cake. After completing the piped design on the cake, arrange icing flowers and other hand-made or commercial decorations in place, finally fixing them with a little icing when you are satisfied with the effect. The *position of pillars* should be established when the design is being planned, but the pillars themselves are best fixed in position at the end, otherwise they will hinder piping.

On the day Assemble the cake at the reception and arrange fresh flowers in the vase on the top of the cake, if used.

After the wedding Wrap the top tier and any left-over cake in greaseproof paper and then in foil. Store for up to 2 months in a cool dry place. If kept any longer, mould may develop between the almond paste and cake.

If the top tier is to be kept for a christening cake, it should be stripped of almond paste and icing and stored as above. It should be re-iced shortly before it is required.

Icing a formal cake

Quantities
The amount of almond paste quoted will give a thin layer. The amount of royal icing should be enough to give 2 coats plus simple decorations.

Square tin size		15 cm (6 in) square	18 cm (7 in) square	20·5 cm (8 in) square	23 cm (9 in) square	25·5 cm (10 in) square	28 cm (11 in) square	30·5 cm (12 in) square
Round tin size	15 cm (6 in) round	18 cm (7 in) round	20·5 cm (8 in) round	23 cm (9 in) round	25·5 cm (10 in) round	28 cm (11 in) round	30·5 cm (12 in) round	
Almond paste	350 g (¾ lb)	450 g (1 lb)	550 g (1¼ lb)	800 g (1¾ lb)	900 g (2 lb)	1 kg (2¼ lb)	1·1 kg (2½ lb)	1·4 kg (3 lb)
Royal icing	450 g (1 lb)	550 g (1¼ lb)	700 g (1½ lb)	900 g (2 lb)	1 kg (2¼ lb)	1·1 kg (2½ lb)	1·4 kg (3 lb)	1·6 kg (3½ lb)

Lily-of-the-valley wedding cake (1-tier)

Illustrated on the jacket

You will need:
28-cm (11-in) round cake covered in almond
    paste on a 35·5-cm (14-in) round cake board
kneaded white fondant icing using 900 g (2 lb)
    icing sugar etc.
egg white
white royal icing using 700 g (1½ lb) icing
    sugar etc.

Decoration
silver balls and leaves
fabric sprigs of lily-of-the-valley
small fresh or fabric flowers for
    centre arrangement

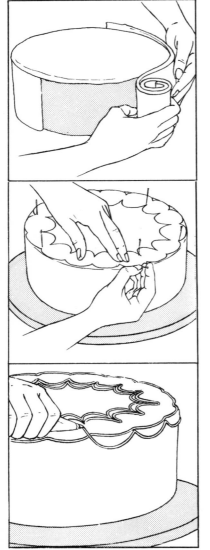

Measure the outer edge of the cake with a piece of string. Divide the fondant icing into three equal pieces. Roll two pieces the depth of the side of the cake and half the length of the string. Roll the third piece into a circle the size of the top of the cake. Brush the almond paste with lightly beaten egg white and place the round of fondant in position. Trim away any excess icing. Roll the two strips of icing loosely and apply to the side of the cake. Trim away any excess icing and mould the top edge and side joins. Leave to dry for about 24 hours.

Make a greaseproof paper template the size of the top of the cake and draw in 16 even sized scallops. Place in position and secure with a number of pins. Prick out the inner and outer scallop edge on to the cake with a pin. Make sure the pin pricks are clear before removing the greaseproof paper.

Using an icing bag fitted with a plain nozzle (No. 2), pipe along the outline of the inner and outer scalloped edge. Pipe a second line on top of the first. Pipe a looped edge under the outer scalloped edge, allowing the icing to form loops on the side of the cake. Pipe a second line on top of the first. Using an icing bag fitted with a plain nozzle (No. 1), pipe a line inside the inner scalloped edge.

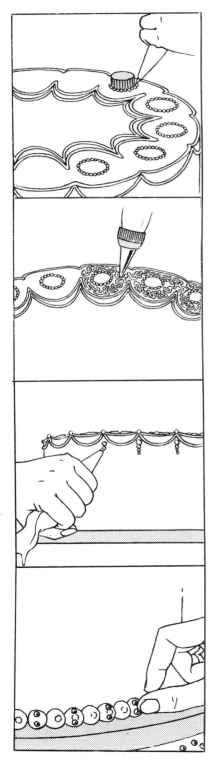

Use a 2·5-cm (1-in) round bottle cap or pastry cutter as a template. Place in the centre of each scallop. Using an icing bag fitted with a plain nozzle (No. 2), pipe a ring of dots around the cap, making sure the icing does not actually touch the cap. Remove the cap and repeat in the centre of each scallop on the top of the cake.

Using an icing bag fitted with a plain nozzle (No. 1), pipe lace around the outside of the circle of dots and inside the scalloped edge. Hold the top of the pipe close to the surface of the cake and move the nozzle in a continuous wiggly line. Repeat the lace in each scallop section.

Using an icing bag fitted with a plain nozzle (No. 3), pipe a small dot at the join of each scallop on the side of the cake. Using the same nozzle, pipe a larger dot underneath with three more dots, decreasing in size. Repeat the dots all around the side of the cake.
  Using the same nozzle, pipe a dot in the centre of alternate scallops. Place five silver balls around the iced dot before the dot dries — to look like a flower.

Using an icing bag fitted with a plain nozzle (No. 3), pipe a border of large dots at the base of the cake. Place two silver balls on each alternate dot.
  Place little sprigs of lily-of-the-valley in each alternate scallop and secure with a little icing. Place the centre piece on top of the cake and, if needed, secure with a little icing underneath the base.

Daisy wedding cake (2-tier)

You will need:
28-cm (11-in) square cake covered in almond
    paste on a 38-cm (15-in) square cake board
18-cm (7-in) square cake covered in almond
    paste on a 20·5-cm (8-in) square cake board
white royal icing using 2 kg (4½ lb) icing
    sugar etc.

Decoration
four 7·5-cm (3-in) pillars
about 200 piped daisies (see page 30)
40 silver leaves
ribbon

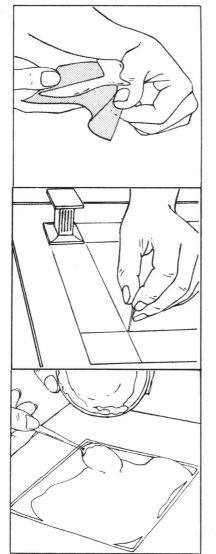

Flat ice the two cakes with royal icing. Leave to dry for 24 hours and then apply a second coat of icing. Leave to dry for at least 24 hours (see page 19). To make the run-out corner wings, draw the shape on greaseproof paper squaring the inner corners. Cover with non-stick or waxed paper and pipe in the outline with an icing bag fitted with a plain nozzle (No. 2). Thin some icing a little and flood the corner wings easing the icing into the corners with a skewer or cocktail stick. Make six small and six large corners (extra in case of breakages) and leave to dry for several days. Carefully peel away the non-stick paper.

Cut a piece of thin card or greaseproof paper the size of the top of the base cake. Position the pillars so they are inside the corners of the smaller cake board. Draw parallel lines from pillar to pillar from inner and outer corners. Remove the pillars. Position the template on the cake and prick through the position of the pillars with a pin.

Using an icing bag fitted with a plain nozzle (No. 2), pipe a square on the top of the base cake by joining the four inner pinprick marks. Spoon some thinned royal icing into the square, easing it into the corners with a skewer or cocktail stick. Quickly prick any air bubbles and leave to dry.

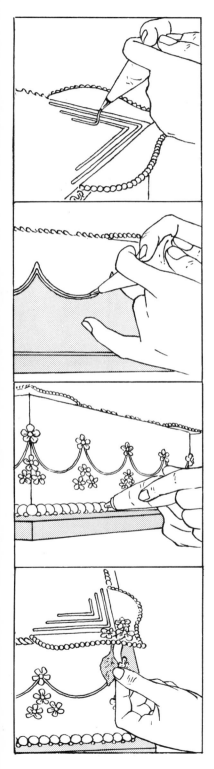

Spread a little icing on the underside of each wing and on each corner of the cakes. Carefully position the smaller wings on the top cake and the larger ones on the base cake. Using an icing bag fitted with a plain nozzle (No. 2), pipe a close row of tiny dots around the outside edge of each wing. Pipe a rope effect line on the top edge of the cake between the wings. Outline the inner edge of each corner with three right-angled graduated lines.

Cut two templates to fit the sides of both cakes. Divide the base template and cut out four scallops of equal shape using a glass or pastry cutter as a guide. Divide the top template and cut out three scallops in the same way. Place the template in position and outline the scallops following the line of the template with a plain nozzle (No. 2). Remove the template and repeat on all sides.

Fix a daisy where the scallops meet and a group of three daisies just below on the sides of the cake. Using an icing bag fitted with a plain nozzle (No. 3), pipe large dots close together around the base of the cake. With the plain nozzle (No. 2), pipe a tiny dot between each large dot. Repeat on all sides of both tiers. Group three daisies in the centre of each corner. Place a group of three daisies between each pillar and pipe in three radiating lines. Place three daisies in the centre of the 'flooded' square and pipe in three radiating lines.

On the top tier, place a group of three daisies on two opposite sides. Pipe in two radiating lines. Place a pair of silver leaves at the base and top of each corner. Place the pillars in position on the base cake. Pleat the ribbon as shown and secure with pins to hold in place. Place on the top cake and secure with a little icing. Do not store the cake assembled but keep the tiers separately.

Lace-iced wedding cake (3-tier)

You will need:
three round cakes of the following sizes covered
    in almond paste: 30·5-cm (12-in), 23-cm
    (9-in), 15-cm (6-in) on three round cake
    boards: 40·5-cm (16-in), 28-cm (11-in),
    20·5-cm (8-in)
white royal icing using 2·7 kg (6 lb) icing
    sugar etc.

Decoration
four 9-cm (3½-in) and 7·5-cm (3-in) round pillars
silver balls and small white fabric flowers
100 piped daisies (see page 30)
8 silver horseshoes
small silver vase with fresh flowers

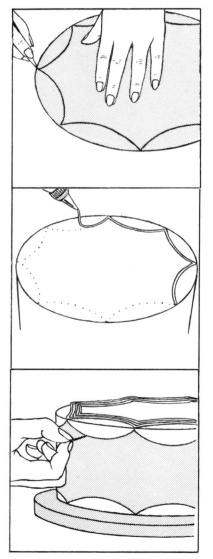

Flat ice the cakes with two coats of royal icing (see page 19). Place the pillars in position on the base and middle cakes and prick round them to ensure the design does not cover these spaces. Cut a circle of thin card or greaseproof paper the size of the top of each cake. Fold the large and middle sized ones into eight and the top one into six. Either using a compass or the base of a suitable size glass, mark in the scallops between the folds in the paper, about 2·5 cm (1 in) at the deepest part for the bottom two layers and 1 cm (½ in) deep for the top tier. Cut out the scallops.

Place the paper on the cake and secure with pins. Prick the outline of the scallops on the top of each cake. Remove the paper. Using an icing bag fitted with a plain nozzle (No. 2), outline the scallops following the marked lines. Using an icing bag fitted with a plain nozzle (No. 3), pipe a line outlining the scallop 0·5 cm (¼ in) outside the first. Using the plain nozzle (No. 2), pipe a third line 0·5 cm (¼ in) outside the thicker line.

To mark the scallops on the side of the cake, measure the depth of the cake and cut a band of greaseproof paper to size. Place it round the cake and secure with pins. Mark the points of each scallop already piped on top of the cake. Remove the paper and draw in and cut out the scallops as for the top. At the same time, draw corresponding scallops 1 cm (½ in) deep at the base. Secure the paper round the cake and prick out the design.

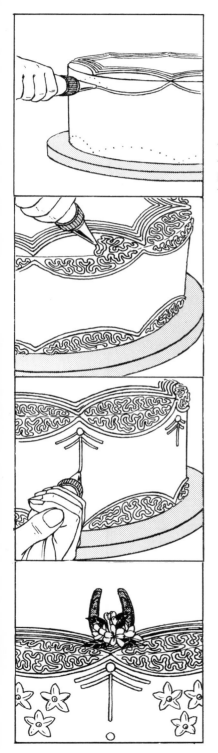

Tilt the cake slightly and rest it on a firmly wedged shallow tin so that you can work on the sides easily. Using an icing bag fitted with a plain nozzle (No. 2), pipe in the scallops at the top and bottom of the sides of the cakes.

Fill in the scallops on the top, sides and base of the cake with a lace effect. Using an icing bag fitted with a plain nozzle (No. 2), pipe a continuous wiggly line without making a set pattern. The nozzle should be held quite close to the surface of the cake while icing lace.

Using an icing bag fitted with a plain nozzle (No. 3), pipe in two fern-shaped lines on the side of the cake 0·5 cm ($\frac{1}{4}$ in) below the side scallop. Pipe the second line 0·5 cm ($\frac{1}{4}$ in) below the first line with the plain nozzle (No. 2) then pipe the vertical line. Pipe a dot at the top of the fern, where all the lines meet.

Using an icing bag fitted with a plain nozzle (No. 3), pipe large dots round the base of the bottom tier. Use the plain nozzle (No. 2) to pipe the dots round the base of the middle and top tiers. Using the plain nozzle (No. 3), pipe three dots decreasing in size at the point of the scallops at the base of the cake. Place a silver ball on the bottom dot. Position the pillars and daisies, securing with a little icing. Pipe a small dot in the centre of each daisy and top with a silver ball. Place the fabric flowers and horseshoes on top of the cake and secure with a little icing. Place the vase and flowers in position.

Silver vase wedding cake (3-tier)

Illustrated in colour facing page 88

You will need:
three square cakes of the following sizes covered
   in almond paste: 30·5-cm (12-in), 23-cm
   (9-in), 15-cm (6-in) on three square cake
   boards: 40·5-cm (16-in), 28-cm (11-in),
   20·5-cm (8-in)
white royal icing using 3·2 kg (7 lb) icing
   sugar etc.

Decoration
silver balls
12 small corner silver vases
asparagus fern and sea heather
four 9-cm (3½-in), 7·5-cm (3-in) square pillars
small silver vase with fresh flowers

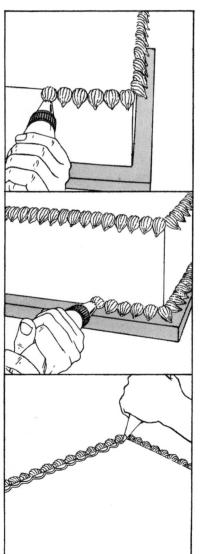

Flat ice the three cakes with royal icing. Leave to dry for
about 24 hours and then apply a second coat of icing. Leave
to dry for at least 24 hours (see page 19). Using an icing bag
fitted with a shell nozzle, pipe a border of large shells around
the top edge of the cake with the shell points towards the
outside edge of the cake. Shape the tip of each shell into a
well formed point and at the same time lift away from the
cake — this may need to be done carefully with the finger tips.

Using the icing bag fitted with the shell nozzle, pipe a border
of large shells at the base of the cake with the shell points
towards the edge of the cake board. The tips of the shell
should almost reach the edge of the cake board. Shape the
tips of the shells into well formed points as above. Pipe the
corner shells a little longer.

Using an icing bag fitted with a plain nozzle (No. 3), pipe a
looped border inside the shell edge on the top of the cake.
Place a silver ball at the join of each loop before the icing
dries. Pipe a looped border above the shell edge at the base
of the cake. Place a silver ball at the join of each loop before
the icing dries. (Use a pair of small tweezers to position the
silver balls exactly.)

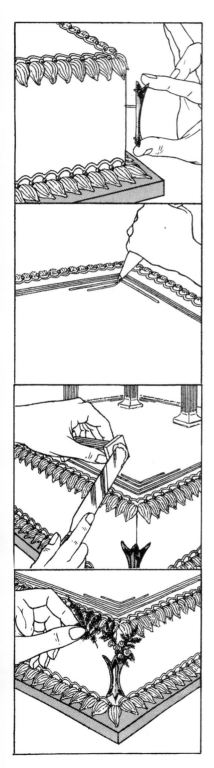

Position the small silver vases on the four corners of the three cakes. If the icing on the cake is very firm, pierce a hole in the correct position on each corner with a fine skewer and then position the vases, allowing plenty of room for the fern and heather to be added later.

Using an icing bag fitted with a plain nozzle (No. 2), pipe a straight line inside the loops on the top of the cake. Leave to dry and pipe a second line on top of the first. Pipe a single line inside the double line. Pipe two right-angled lines in each corner, one a little shorter than the other.

Place the four 9-cm (3½-in) pillars on the base of the cake, ensuring that they are square with each other and the sides of the cake. Secure in place with a little icing. Repeat with the four smaller pillars on the centre cake. Assemble the cake for a trial run but do not leave assembled.

On the day of the wedding select two pieces of fern and one piece of sea heather for each silver vase on the corners of the cakes. Select larger pieces for the bottom tier, slightly smaller for the centre and top tiers. Arrange the fern and heather, making sure the stalks do not protrude at the side of the vases. Arrange the cakes on top of each other and place the small vase of fresh flowers on the top tier.

More simple wedding cake designs

Horseshoe wedding cake (2-tier)

You will need:
28-cm (11-in) round cake covered in almond
paste on a 38-cm (15-in) round cake board
18-cm (7-in) round cake covered in almond paste
on a 20.5-cm (8-in) round cake board
white royal icing using 1.7 kg (3¾ lb) icing
sugar etc.

Decoration
8 silver horseshoe and heather decorations
8 silver horseshoe decorations
three 7.5-cm (3-in) round pillars
silver vase with silver leaves and fabric flowers

Flat ice the cakes with royal icing (see page 19 for
directions). Using an icing bag fitted with an eight
point star nozzle, pipe an alternate shell border
around the top edge of both cakes (see page 29).
Pipe a shell border at the base of both cakes (see
page 28). Using an icing bag fitted with a plain
nozzle (No. 2), pipe a row of three dots on the side
of the cakes under each alternate shell.

Arrange both the horseshoe decorations around
the side of the cake, securing with icing. Place the
pillars in position and pipe dots around the base of
each. Place the silver vase with flowers and leaves
in position and pipe dots around the base.

Silver ribbon wedding cake (3-tier)

You will need:
three round cakes of the following sizes covered in
almond paste: 30.5-cm (12-in), 23-cm (9-in),
15-cm (6-in) on three round cake boards:
40.5-cm (16-in), 28-cm (11-in), 20.5-cm
(8-in)
white royal icing using 2.7 kg (6 lb) icing
sugar etc.

Decoration
2.5-cm (1-in) wide silver cake ribbon
four 9-cm (3½-in) and 7.5-cm (3-in) round pillars
16 small silver leaves
vase and flowers cake decoration

Flat ice the cakes with royal icing (see page 19 for
directions). Place the silver ribbon around the centre
of each cake and secure with a little icing.

Using an icing bag fitted with an eight point star
nozzle, pipe a star border around the top and bottom
edges of each cake with the stars spaced evenly.
Pipe a second star border exactly underneath the
top border and another row above the bottom
border. Using an icing bag fitted with a plain nozzle
(No. 2), pipe a zig-zag line connecting the centres
of alternate stars (see pages 27–28). Place the pillars
in position and pipe stars around the base of each.
Pipe a larger star between each pillar and place a
silver leaf either side. Place the vase of flowers on
the top tier.

1st anniversary cake (*page 91*).
Engagement cake (*page 90*)

Butterfly wedding cake (3-tier)

You will need:
three square cakes of the following sizes covered
   in almond paste: 30·5-cm (12-in), 23-cm
   (9-in), 15-cm (6-in) on three square cake
   boards: 40·5-cm (16-in), 28-cm (11-in),
   20·5-cm (8-in)
white royal icing using 3·2 kg (7 lb) icing
   sugar etc.

Decoration
12 silver leaf and flower decorations
four 9-cm (3½-in) and 7·5-cm (3-in) square pillars
butterfly and flower cake decoration

Flat ice the cakes with royal icing (see page 19 for
directions). Using an icing bag fitted with an eight
point star nozzle, pipe a zig-zag border around the
top and bottom edge of each cake (see page 28).
Using the same nozzle, pipe a zig-zag border down
the corner of each cake. Pipe a small star at the
base of each corner.

Using an icing bag fitted with a plain nozzle
(No. 2), pipe a row of dots in a rectangle on the
sides of all the cakes. Using the same nozzle, pipe a
row of dots in a square on the top surfaces of the
cakes.

Place a leaf and flower decoration at each corner
and secure in place with a little icing. Place the
pillars in position and secure with a little icing.

Place the butterfly and flower decoration on the
top tier.

Silver shoe wedding cake (2-tier)

You will need:
28-cm (11-in) square cake covered in almond
   paste on a 38-cm (15-in) square cake board
18-cm (7-in) square cake covered in almond paste
   on a 20·5-cm (8-in) square cake board
white royal icing using 2 kg (4½ lb) icing
   sugar etc.

Decoration
8 silver shoe and flower decorations
8 silver leaf and flower decorations
four 7·5-cm (3-in) square pillars
4 silver horseshoes
horseshoe and flower cake decoration

Flat ice the cakes with royal icing (see page 19 for
directions). Using an icing bag fitted with an eight
point star nozzle, pipe a shell border around the top
and bottom edges of both cakes (see page 28).
Using the same nozzle, pipe a shell border down
each corner of the cakes. At the base of each corner,
pipe a large shell so the point reaches the edge of
the board.

Place a silver shoe decoration at each top corner
and secure in place with a little icing. Position a
leaf and flower decoration in the centre of each side
and secure in place with a little icing.

Arrange the four pillars and secure in place with a
little icing. Pipe a rosette between each pillar and
place a horseshoe in the centre of each. Position the
horseshoe and flower decoration on the top tier.

Baby girl's novelty christening cake (*page 94*),
Cradle christening cake (*page 95*)

Birthday cakes

Apricot ribbon cake

Illustrated on the jacket

You will need:
23-cm (9-in) round cake covered in almond
   paste on a 28-cm (11-in) round cake board
white royal icing using 900 g (2 lb) icing
   sugar etc.
green food colouring
apricot food colouring

Decoration
2·5-cm (1-in) wide green ribbon
0·5-cm (¼-in) wide apricot ribbon
apricot fabric flower

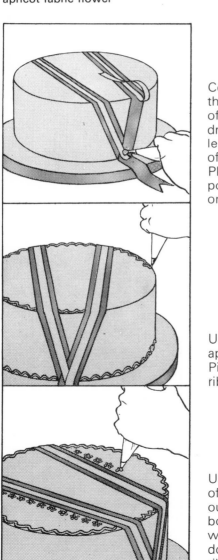

Colour 45 ml (3 tbsp) royal icing green and reserve. Colour the remaining icing a deep apricot. Flat ice the top and side of the cake and the cake board with apricot icing. Leave to dry for about 24 hours. Using a piece of thread, measure the length of ribbon required: allow for one side, across the top of the cake, down the other side plus 5–7 cm (2–3 in) extra. Place two pieces of green ribbon to form a 'V' and secure in position with a little icing. Place two pieces of apricot ribbon on top of the green and secure in position with a little icing.

Using an icing bag fitted with a plain nozzle (No. 3) and apricot icing, pipe a looped border around the base edge. Pipe a looped border around the top edge but not over the ribbons and leave to dry.

Using the same icing bag filled with apricot icing, pipe a row of daisies – circles of four or five even sized dots – along the outside edges of the ribbon. Pipe daisies around the cake board grouped in twos or threes. Using an icing bag fitted with a plain nozzle (No. 3) and green icing, pipe a centre dot in each daisy. Place the fabric flower at the join of the ribbon on the side of the cake and secure with a little icing.

Rosebud cake

Illustrated in colour facing page 49

You will need:
23-cm (9-in) round cake covered in almond
    paste on a 28-cm (11-in) round cake board
pale green royal icing using 900 g (2 lb) icing
    sugar etc.
white royal icing using 225 g (8 oz) icing
    sugar etc.

Decoration
embroidered flower edging
white ribbon

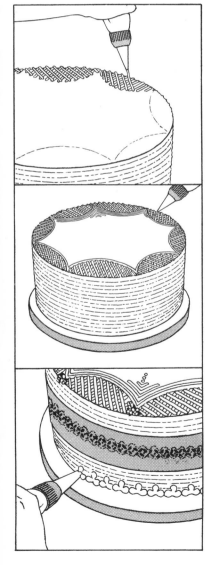

Flat ice the top and side of the cake with green icing. Finish the sides with a rib effect by using a serrated icing comb. Then leave to dry for about 24 hours. Flat ice the edge of the cake board with green icing and leave to dry for about 24 hours. Using a template, mark the top of the cake into eight even scallops (see page 35). Using an icing bag fitted with a plain nozzle (No. 2) and white icing, pipe a trellis in each scallop.

Using the same nozzle, pipe a line along the inner edge of the scallops. Using an icing bag fitted with a plain nozzle (No. 1) and white icing, pipe a line inside the scalloped edge. Pipe two V's and three dots at the join of each scallop.

Cut eight embroidered flowers from the edging. Place the ribbon in position around the cake and place the remaining embroidered edging on top. Secure in position with a little icing. Position a flower at the join of each scallop on top of the cake with a little icing. Using an icing bag fitted with a three point star nozzle and white icing, pipe a star border (see page 29) around the base of the cake.

Basket birthday cake

Illustrated in colour facing page 49

You will need:
23-cm (9-in) round cake covered in almond
 paste on a 28-cm (11-in) round cake board
white royal icing using 900 g (2 lb) icing
 sugar etc.

Decoration
cane or wire plaited handle sprayed silver
white and silver ribbon
fresh flowers and fern

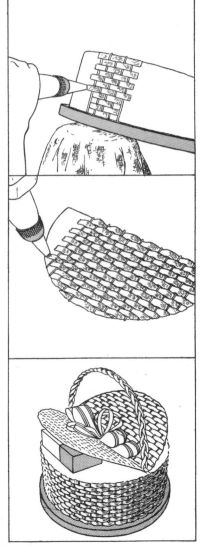

Flat ice the top and side of the cake with the royal icing and leave to dry for 24 hours. Fill two icing bags with icing, one fitted with a plain nozzle (No. 2), the other with a basket nozzle. Pipe vertical lines down the side of the cake. Pipe short horizontal lines using the basket pipe, spaced evenly over the vertical lines (see page 29). Continue round the side of the cake and leave to dry for about 24 hours.

Cut a circle of white cardboard slightly smaller than the top of the cake and cut in half. Cover both pieces with basket effect piping and leave to dry for about 24 hours.

Pipe a thick line of icing down the centre of the cake and position the two 'lids' in place, supporting them while they dry. Secure the handle in place with a little icing. Tie the ribbon into a bow almost the width of the cake and place in the centre of the lid. On the day of serving, arrange the flowers and fern in the 'basket'.

Apricot mother birthday cake

Illustrated in colour facing page 64

You will need:
23-cm (9-in) square cake covered in almond
  paste on a 28-cm (11-in) square cake board
apricot royal icing using 1 kg (2¼ lb) icing
  sugar etc.

Decoration
narrow apricot ribbon
14 apricot fondant roses (see page 36)
spray of small apricot fabric flowers

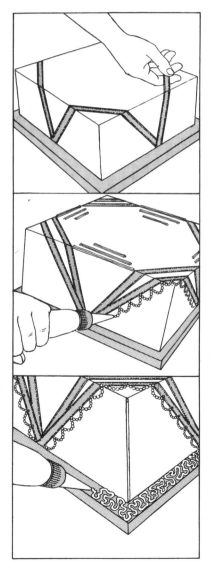

Flat ice the top and sides of the cake with the royal icing and leave to dry for about 24 hours. Place a double row of ribbon in position, securing in the centre of each side with a pin at the base edge.

Using an icing bag fitted with a plain nozzle (No. 2), pipe two straight lines, touching each other, along the top edges between the ribbon. Pipe another straight line on top of the two lines. Repeat these lines twice, decreasing in length. Pipe two straight lines down each corner then pipe a single line on top. Pipe a series of small dots in a scalloped pattern along the ribbon edge. Arrange the flowers in position and secure in place with a little icing.

Using the icing bag fitted with the plain nozzle (No. 2), pipe a lace effect on the board by piping a continuous wiggly line. Do not make a set pattern but keep the spaces an even size. Pipe 'Mother' on the top of the cake.
  Place a single rose in the centre at the base of each side and secure with a little icing.

18 Birthday cake

You will need:
23-cm (9-in) square cake covered in almond
    paste on a 28-cm (11-in) square cake board
white royal icing using 1 kg (2½ lb) icing
    sugar etc.
blue royal icing using 225 g (8 oz) icing
    sugar etc.

Decoration
silver balls
white ribbon
blue fabric flowers
4 silver keys

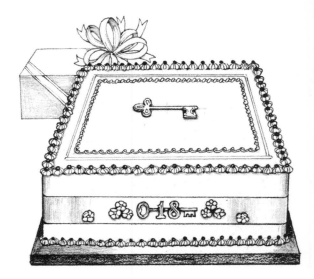

To make the run-out key, draw a decorative key about 6 cm (2 in) long on a piece of non-stick or waxed paper. Using an icing bag fitted with a plain nozzle (No. 2) and white icing, pipe around the outline. Using a greaseproof icing bag without a nozzle, flood the key, easing the icing into the corners with a skewer or cocktail stick. Leave to dry for 24–48 hours before carefully peeling off paper. Flat ice the top and sides of the cake with white icing and leave to dry for about 24 hours.

Using an icing bag fitted with an eight point star nozzle, pipe white rosettes around the top and bottom edges of the cake. Top each with a silver ball. Using an icing bag fitted with a plain nozzle (No. 2) and white icing, pipe a straight line inside the rosettes along each side.

Using an icing bag fitted with a plain nozzle (No. 2), pipe a continuous line of blue 'loops' inside the white line. Place the ribbon in position around the cake and secure the flowers and a silver key on the ribbon. Place the run-out key in the centre of the cake and secure with a little icing.

Clown cake

Illustrated in colour facing page 89

You will need:
23-cm (9-in) round cake covered in almond
    paste on a 28-cm (11-in) round cake board
225 g (8 oz) almond paste
yellow royal icing using 900 g (2 lb) icing
    sugar etc.
green food colouring
orange food colouring
red food colouring

Decoration
commercial clown decoration
candles and candle holders

Divide the almond paste in half and roll out thinly. Using a fluted pastry cutter, cut four 3·5-cm (1½-in) circles. Cut each in half and trim to make the ruffs. Using a plain cutter, cut eight 2·5-cm (1-in) circles for the heads. Cut eight small triangles and eight small strips for hats. Colour 50 g (2 oz) of the remaining almond paste green and roll out. Using a plain pastry cutter, cut eight 3·5-cm (1½-in) circles for bodies. Colour 50 g (2 oz) paste orange and roll out. Cut sixteen small triangles for feet and mould thin strips for hair. Colour the remaining piece red for buttons and noses. Pipe eyes and mouths.

Flat ice the top and side of the cake with the yellow icing and leave to dry for about 24 hours. Spread a little icing on the back of each piece of the clown and place in position on the side of the cake. Using an icing bag fitted with a plain nozzle (No. 3), pipe large yellow dots around the top and bottom edges of the cake. Using a dampened finger, gently flatten the peaks of the dots if necessary.

Using the same nozzle write 'Happy Birthday' on the cake. (Use a template and prick out the letters on the cake first if you are unsure about piping straight on· to the cake.) Place the clown decoration in position and stick to the cake with a little icing. Place the candles and holders behind the hat of each almond paste clown.

Owl and pussycat book

Illustrated in colour facing page 89

You will need:

20·5×28-cm (8×10-in) rectangular cake
  covered in almond paste on a 30·5-cm (12-in)
  square cake board
instant coffee powder
kneaded fondant icing using 900 g (2 lb) icing
  sugar etc.
egg white
cocoa powder, sieved
white royal icing using 225 g (8 oz) icing
  sugar etc.

Decoration
ribbon

Cut a diagonal wedge, about 6 cm (1½ in) wide at the top, from the centre of the cake – to form the fold in the pages. Cut a small half circle on both long sides, underneath the diagonal cut – to form the spine of the book. Dissolve 5–10 ml (1–2 level tsp) instant coffee powder in a little warm water. Knead a little at a time into the fondant icing until the desired beige colour is achieved.

Roll out two-thirds of the fondant icing thinly on a surface dusted with sifted icing sugar. Cut into two lengths 25·5×7·5 cm (10×3 in) and two lengths 20·5×7·5 cm (8×3 in). Brush the cake sides with lightly beaten egg white and cover with the fondant. Trim away the excess icing and reserve a little for the animal decoration. Mark in lines for the pages on all four sides. Roll out the remaining fondant to a rectangle about 30·5×20·5 cm (12×8 in). Brush the top of the cake with egg white and place the fondant in position. Trim away the excess icing.

Knead a little cocoa powder into the remaining fondant icing trimmings. Roll out thinly and cut into two strips 51 cm (20 in) long and 2·5 cm (1 in) wide. Place around the book on the board. Fold into a loose pleat at the centre of each long side. Colour the trimmings and use to make the animal shapes. Leave the cake and animals to dry for about 24 hours. Using an icing bag fitted with a plain nozzle (No. 2), pipe a white line around the edge of the book. Write in the rhyme and the page numbers. Decorate the animals and place in position. Arrange the ribbon as a book mark down the centre and secure with a little icing.

Opposite Silver vase wedding cake (3-tier) (*page 78*).
Overleaf Santa and sleigh cake (*page 100*), Christmas rose cake (*page 101*), Christmas tree cake (*page 98*), American frosted Christmas cake (*page 99*)

Pink elephant cake

Illustrated in colour opposite

You will need:
23-cm (9-in) square cake covered in almond
    paste on a 25·5-cm (10-in) square cake board
white royal icing using 1 kg (2¼ lb) icing
    sugar etc.
pink kneaded fondant icing using 450 g (1 lb)
    icing sugar etc.
pink royal icing using 225 g (8 oz) icing
    sugar etc.

Flat ice the top and sides of the cake with the white royal icing. Leave to dry for about 24 hours. To shape the elephants for the sides of the cake, roll out two-thirds of the fondant icing on a surface dusted with sifted icing sugar. Cut four 5-cm (2-in) circles and cut out a 2·5-cm (1-in) square from each to shape the body. Repeat cutting four 3·5-cm (1½-in) circles for smaller elephants. Cut four 3·5-cm (1½-in) circles and four 2·5-cm (1-in) circles for the heads. Shape the trimmings into trunks and ears. Assemble, sticking together with a little icing, and pipe in the tusks, eyes and feet with white icing.

Divide the remaining fondant icing in half and shape into the large elephant. Shape two-thirds into a cylinder and bend in half to form the legs and body. Roll a ball for the head and pull out the trunk. Shape the ears and tail from the trimmings. Leave to dry in an upright position, with the trunk supported, for 24 hours. Repeat, making two smaller elephants with the remaining fondant icing. Assemble, sticking together with a little icing and pipe in the tusks, eyes and feet with white icing.

Using an icing bag fitted with a plain nozzle (No. 3), pipe large white dots along the top and bottom edges of the cake. Pipe a double line of dots down each corner and leave to dry for about 1 hour. Using an icing bag fitted with a plain nozzle (No. 2), pipe a small pink dot on the top of each white dot and leave to dry for 1 hour. Pipe 'Happy Birthday' in pink directly on the top of the cake. Position all the elephants and secure in place with a little icing. Using the bag filled with white icing, pipe a loop between alternate pink dots along the top edge.

Pink elephant cake (*page 89*), Clown cake (*page 87*),
Owl and pussycat book (*page 88*)

Anniversary and christening cakes

Engagement cake

Illustrated in colour facing page 80

You will need:

23-cm (9-in) heart-shaped cake covered in almond paste on a heart-shaped cake board
pink royal icing using 900 g (2 lb) icing sugar
lilac royal icing using 450 g (1 lb) icing sugar etc.
white royal icing using 225 g (8 oz) icing sugar etc.

Decoration
white ribbon
pink fabric rosebuds
silver heart decoration

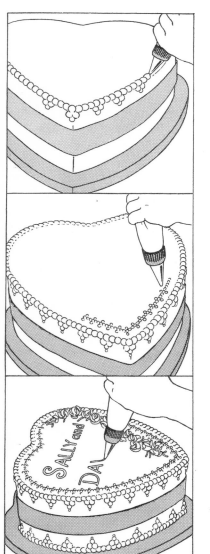

Flat ice the top and sides of the cake with pink icing and leave to dry for about 24 hours. Place the ribbon in position and secure with a pin. Using an icing bag fitted with a plain nozzle (No. 3), pipe a line of lilac dots around the top and bottom edge. At evenly spaced intervals, pipe a group of three dots on the top and bottom border.

Using an icing bag fitted with a plain nozzle (No. 2), pipe a row of white dots inside the top lilac edging. Pipe a dot either side of every fourth dot in the row.

Place the rosebuds and silver heart in position and secure with a little icing. Using the icing bag fitted with the plain nozzle (No. 2), pipe a few short white lines amongst the roses. Using the same nozzle, pipe the names of the couple in white on the top of the cake.

1st Anniversary cake

Illustrated in colour facing page 80

You will need:
23-cm (9-in) round cake covered in almond
    paste on a 28-cm (11-in) round cake board
yellow royal icing using 900 g (2 lb) icing
    sugar etc.
white royal icing using 450 g (1 lb) icing
    sugar etc.

Decoration
spray of small white fabric flowers
doves and ring decoration

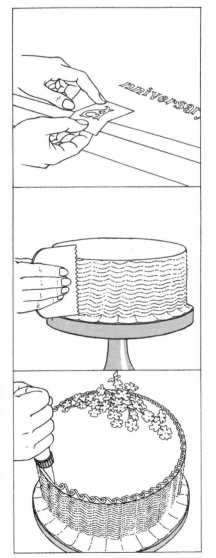

Draw or trace stylised lettering on a piece of non-stick or waxed paper. Using an icing bag fitted with a plain nozzle (No. 2) and white icing, pipe around the outline of the letters. Using the same nozzle, flood the letters, easing the icing into the corners with a skewer or cocktail stick. Leave to dry for about 24–48 hours before carefully peeling off the paper over the edge of a table. Make extra letters in case of breakages. Flat ice the top and side of the cake with yellow icing and leave to dry for about 24 hours.

Spread white icing around the side of the cake and smooth roughly. Using a serrated icing comb, rib the side of the cake, moving the comb up and down the side evenly. Press firmly enough to reveal the yellow icing. The wavy effect on the cake board is achieved with this movement at the same time as ribbing the side of the cakes. Leave to dry for about 24 hours.

Using an icing bag fitted with a plain nozzle (No. 2), pipe a border of small scrolls along the top edge. Arrange the flowers, lettering and decoration in place and secure with a little icing.

Silver anniversary cake

Illustrated in colour facing page 65

You will need:

20·5×28-cm (8×10-in) rectangular cake covered
 in almond paste diagonally placed on a 28-cm
 (11-in) square cake board
white royal icing using 1 kg (2¼ lb) icing
 sugar etc.

Decoration
piped daisies and roses (see page 30)
silver balls and 26 silver leaves
silver cake ribbon
two run-out 25 numbers (see page 34)
white satin fabric roses

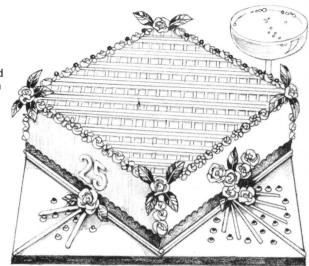

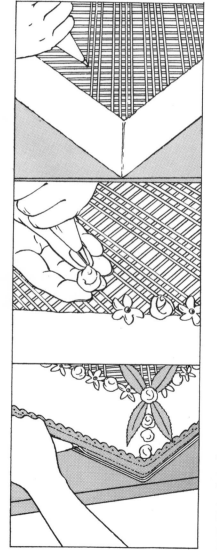

Flat ice the top and sides of the cake with white icing and
leave to dry for about 24 hours. Using an icing bag fitted with
a plain nozzle (No. 3) and white icing, pipe even spaced
lines diagonally across the top of the cake. Leave to dry for
about 30 minutes. Turn the cake and pipe the second layer
of lines at right angles to the first – pipe groups of four
evenly spaced straight lines. Leave a gap of about 1 cm (½ in)
between each group to give a plaid effect trellis icing.

Place the silver ribbon around the base of the cake and
secure with a little icing. Place the piped daisies and roses
alternately around the top edge of the cake, securing each
with a little icing. Pipe a dot in the centre of each daisy and
top with a silver ball. Arrange piped roses in a row down
each corner with four silver leaves. Place the numbers 25 in
the centre of two opposite sides, secure with a little icing.

Using an icing bag fitted with a plain nozzle (No. 3), pipe
two parallel lines along the base edge of each side. Leave to
dry for about 30 minutes and then pipe a single line along
the centre of the two lines. Pipe a series of radiating lines
and dots on the four sections of cake board. Pipe dots
between the lines and top with silver balls. Place the fabric
roses and leaves on the sides of the cake, securing with a
little icing.

Golden anniversary cake

Illustrated in colour facing page 65

You will need:
23-cm (9-in) round cake covered in almond
    paste on a 28-cm (11-in) round gold cake
    board
white royal icing using 900 g (2 lb) icing
    sugar etc.

Decoration
gold gift ribbon
7 sugar bells (see page 43)
gold balls
one run-out 50 number (see page 34)

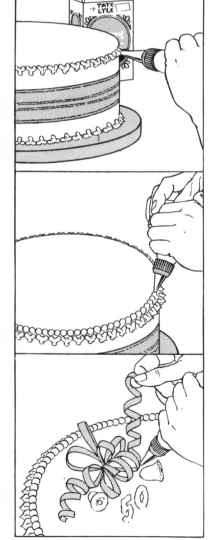

Flat ice the top and side of the cake with white icing and leave to dry for about 24 hours. Place a double row of ribbon around the middle of the cake and secure in position with a little icing. Using an icing bag fitted with a three point star nozzle, pipe a single row of stars around the top and bottom edge.

Using an icing bag fitted with a plain nozzle (No. 3), pipe a line of dots inside the stars on the top edge, gently twisting the nozzle slightly before lifting away from the icing to prevent forming peaks. Cut 4 short pieces of gift ribbon in half lengthways. Form into a group of loops and secure at the base with sewing thread. Cut short lengths of ribbon and make into curls by pulling under the closed blades of a pair of scissors.

Arrange the ribbons in position on the top and sides of the cake. Secure each with a little icing. Pipe a little icing in each bell and top with a gold ball. Place the bells in position and secure with a little icing. Place the numbers on the cake and support in an upright position with a little icing.

Baby girl's novelty christening cake

Illustrated in colour facing page 81

You will need:
23-cm (9-in) square cake covered in almond
   paste on a 28-cm (11-in) square cake board
pink royal icing using 900 g (2 lb) icing
   sugar etc.
white royal icing using 450 g (1 lb) icing
   sugar etc.

Decoration
8 piped flowers (see page 30)
1 fondant mouse and bottle (see page 38)

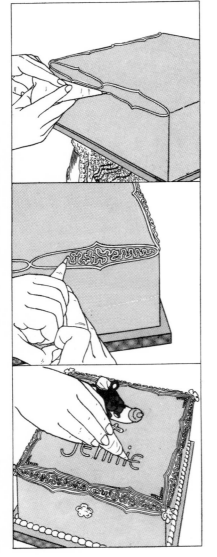

Flat ice the top and sides of the cake with the pink icing and leave to dry for about 24 hours. Draw the outline of safety pins on a piece of non-stick or waxed paper. Using an icing bag fitted with a plain nozzle (No. 2) and white icing, pipe the outline of the safety pins. Using an icing bag fitted with a plain nozzle (No. 2) and pink icing, pipe over the white icing. Leave to dry for 24 hours before carefully removing from the paper. Make a template (see page 35) and mark out the pattern on the top and sides of the cake with a pin. Using the icing bag fitted with a plain nozzle (No. 2), outline the pattern by following the pin pricks on the top and sides of the cake with white icing.

Using the same icing bag, fill each section with 'lace effect' (see page 77). Using an icing bag fitted with a plain nozzle (No. 1), pipe a line inside each section on the top of the cake and under each section on the side of the cake. Using the same icing bag, pipe graduated dots in each corner of the cake.

Using an icing bag fitted with a plain nozzle (No. 2) and white icing, pipe a line of dots along the bottom edge. Place a flower on each corner and one in the centre of each side, secure in place with a little icing. Pipe the name of the baby on the cake. Place the mouse and bottle decoration and safety pin shapes in place, fixing with a little icing.

Cradle christening cake

Illustrated in colour facing page 81

You will need:
23-cm (9-in) round cake covered in almond
    paste on a 28-cm (11-in) round cake board
white royal icing using 225 g (8 oz) icing
    sugar etc.
blue royal icing using 900 g (2 lb) icing
    sugar etc.

Decoration
silver balls
white ribbon
cradle decoration (see note)

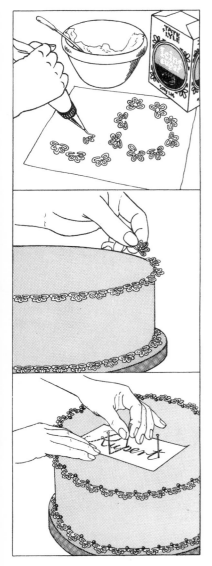

Using an icing bag fitted with a plain nozzle (No. 2) and white icing, pipe the individual pieces of lace on a piece of non-stick or waxed paper. For each piece of lace, pipe five touching loops in a continuous line, then top the centre three with a dot (see page 33). Leave to dry for about 24 hours before carefully peeling off the paper. Make extra in case of breakages. Flat ice the top and side of the cake with blue icing and leave to dry for about 24 hours. Flat ice the board with blue icing and leave to dry for about 24 hours.

Using an icing bag fitted with a plain nozzle (No. 2) and white icing, pipe a line of icing around the top and bottom edge of the cake and place the lace edging on top of this to secure in position. Pipe a dot between each piece of lace and top with a silver ball.

Draw the name of the baby on a piece of greaseproof paper and position it on the top of the cake. Using a pin, prick out the letters on to the cake. Outline the lettering following the pin pricks with a plain nozzle (No. 2) and white icing, and flood the thicker parts of each letter. Position the ribbon and secure with a pin. Place the cradle on the cake and secure with a little icing. Pipe four curved lines from the cradle and fill each with four groups of dots, top with silver balls.

Note The cradle shown on this cake is made from a match box (see page 69). Alternatively make the cradle on page 38.

Festive cakes

Christmas rosette cake

You will need:
23-cm (9-in) round cake covered in almond
   paste on a 28-cm (11-in) round cake board
white royal icing using 900 g (2 lb) icing
   sugar etc.

Decoration
narrow red and green ribbon
red candle
small commercial decoration, e.g. fir cones
wide red ribbon

Flat ice the side of the cake and leave to dry for 24 hours.
Spread icing over the top of the cake and swirl roughly with
a round-bladed knife. Remove any surplus icing from the
side of the cake and then leave to dry for about 24 hours.

Using an icing bag fitted with an eight point star nozzle,
pipe a shell border around the top edge. Pipe a double shell
border around the base edge of the cake.

Make the ribbon rosette with the narrow green and red
ribbon. Tie with thread to hold together and secure in place
with a little icing. Stand the candle in the centre of the
ribbons. Place the wide ribbon around the cake and secure in
place with a pin. Position the fir cones.

Daisy cake (*page 115*), Animal maypole (*page 105*),
Butterfly cake (*page 111*)

Sugar bell Christmas cake

You will need:
23-cm (9-in) round cake covered in almond
    paste on a 28-cm (11-in) round cake board
white royal icing using 900 g (2 lb) icing
    sugar etc.

Decoration
silver balls
12 sugar bells (see page 43)
12 almond paste holly leaves and berries (see
    page 42)
red ribbon

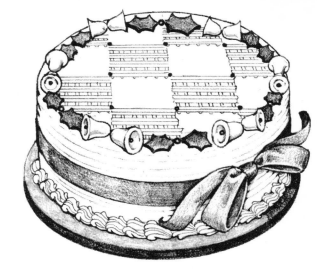

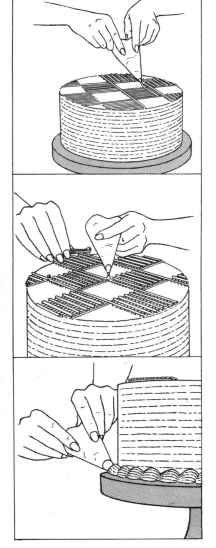

Flat ice the top of the cake with royal icing. Spread icing over the side of the cake and finish with a rib effect by using a serrated icing comb. Leave to dry for about 24 hours. Cut a piece of greaseproof paper the size of the top of the cake and mark into squares. Place the greaseproof paper on top of the cake and prick out the squares with a pin. Using an icing bag fitted with a plain nozzle (No. 2), pipe two layers of trellis in alternate squares.

Using the same icing nozzle, pipe a dot of icing on the corner of each square and top with a silver ball. The easiest way to hold the silver balls and place in the exact position is with a pair of small tweezers.

Using an icing bag fitted with an eight point star nozzle, pipe a shell border around the base edge of the cake. Place the sugar bells and holly leaves around the top edge and secure each in position with a little icing. Place the ribbon around the cake and tie in a bow. Secure in position if necessary with a pin.

Medieval castle (*page 110*)

Christmas tree cake

Illustrated in colour between pages 88 and 89

You will need:
23-cm (9-in) square cake covered in almond
    paste on a 28-cm (11-in) square cake board
white royal icing using 1 kg (2¼ lb) icing
    sugar etc.

Decoration
8 run-out Christmas trees (see page 43)
15 g (½ oz) almond paste
red food colouring
17 silver balls
12 red baubles

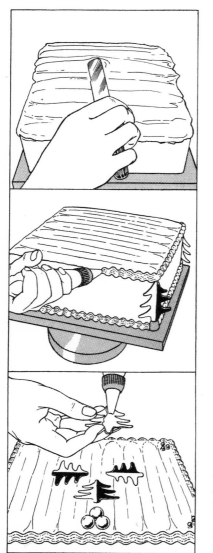

Spoon about half the icing on to the top of the cake and roughly smooth to the edges. Draw a palette knife backwards and forwards across the top of the cake to make evenly spaced 'paddle' marks. Trim away any excess icing at the top edge of the cake and leave to dry for about 24 hours. Coat the sides of the cake with icing and smooth with a palette knife or plain icing comb. Leave to dry for about 24 hours.

Using an icing bag fitted with an eight point star nozzle, pipe the top and bottom borders using a zig-zag motion (see page 28). Pipe a little icing on the back of four Christmas trees and position one at each corner of the cake. Colour the almond paste red and form into four tub shapes for the tree bases. Pipe a little icing on the back of each and place in position under each tree.

Using an icing bag fitted with a plain nozzle (No. 2), pipe three small dots in each corner and five dots in the centre of the cake; top each with a silver ball. Pipe a little icing on the back of each red bauble and position three grouped together in the centre of each top edge. Pipe a little icing on the back of the remaining four trees and arrange on the centre of the cake.

American frosted Christmas cake

Illustrated in colour between pages 88 and 89

You will need:
23-cm (9-in) round cake covered in almond
   paste on a 25-cm (10-in) round cake board
white American frosting using 450 g (1 lb) icing
   sugar etc.
white glacé icing using 100 g (4 oz) icing
   sugar etc.

Decoration
red ribbon with decorative edge
4 small fabric poinsettia decorations
silver balls

American frosting sets quickly so have all your utensils and cake decorations ready before you start. Make up the icing (see page 16) and quickly pour on to the cake. Using a palette knife, spread the icing over the cake, completely covering the almond paste. Using a metal spoon, mark 'swirls' in the icing. Leave to dry for about 1 hour.

Cut a length of ribbon and place in position over the top and sides of the cake. Tie a large bow with the remaining ribbon. Push a pin through the centre of the bow and fix on to the cake.

Using an icing bag fitted with a plain nozzle (No. 2), pipe glacé icing on the back of each flower and place in position on the ribbon. Pipe a number of small dots in a pattern between the flowers and top with silver balls.

Santa and sleigh cake

Illustrated in colour between pages 88 and 89

You will need:
23-cm (9-in) round cake covered in almond
  paste on a 25-cm (10-in) round cake board
royal icing using 900 g (2 lb) icing sugar etc.

Decoration
ribbon
Santa's sleigh:
  8 pipe cleaners
  1 egg white, lightly beaten
  caster sugar
Santa (see page 42)
Christmas tree decoration
2 holly leaves and berries (see page 42)

Spoon the icing on to the top of the cake and roughly
smooth over the top and sides with a palette knife, covering
the almond paste completely. Using the back of a teaspoon
or palette knife, pull the icing into well formed peaks.

Using a palette knife, smooth a path down the centre of the
top and sides of the cake for Santa's sleigh path. Leave to
dry for about 24 hours. Tie a large bow with some of the
ribbon. Place a piece of ribbon on the pathway and the bow
in position.

Bend the pipe cleaners into shape to form the sides of the
sleigh. For the base of the sleigh, wind pipe cleaners
between the two sides. Brush the sleigh with egg white and
dip into sugar. Shake off the excess sugar and leave to dry.
Put Santa and the Christmas tree in the sleigh and place on
the ribbon. Arrange the holly leaves and berries, secure in
place with a little icing.

Christmas rose cake

Illustrated in colour between pages 88 and 89

You will need:
kneaded fondant icing using 900 g (2 lb) icing
    sugar etc.
23-cm (9-in) square cake covered in almond
    paste on a 28-cm (11-in) square cake board
egg white, beaten
royal icing using 225 g (8 oz) icing sugar etc.

Decoration
red ribbon and candle
6 fondant Christmas roses (see page 36)
8 run-out holly leaves and berries
    (see page 33)
2 run-out ivy leaves (see page 33)

Roll out the fondant icing to fit the size of the cake on a surface dusted with icing sugar (see page 21). Brush the almond paste all over with egg white and cover with the fondant. Trim away any surplus fondant and leave to dry for 12–24 hours. Using an icing bag fitted with a plain nozzle (No. 2), pipe three right-angled lines in two opposite corners. Leave to dry for a few minutes and then pipe a second line on top of the first. Pipe a straight line around the top edge of the cake. Leave to dry for a few minutes and then pipe a second line on top of the first.

Using an icing bag fitted with an eight point star nozzle, pipe a shell border along the base edge of the cake.

Place the ribbon around the cake and tie a bow at one corner. Hold in position with a pin if necessary; push the pin through the centre of the bow into the cake.

Arrange the flowers and leaves on the top of the cake. Lift each decoration individually, pipe a little icing on the back and fix on to the cake. Using an icing bag fitted with a plain nozzle (No. 2), pipe lines of dots between the leaves. Pipe a row of dots, graduated in size, in the opposite corners. Pipe a rosette in the centre of the cake and position the candle.

Christmas ring cake

You will need:
23-cm (9-in) round cake
900 g–1·1 kg (2–2½ lb) almond paste
royal icing using 1·4 kg (3 lb) icing sugar etc.
28-cm (11-in) round cake board
12·5-cm (5-in) round cake board

Decoration
ribbon and candle
24 holly leaves and berries (see page 42)
1 Santa (see page 43) or
   6 run-out bells (see page 32)

A week before required, using 800 g (1¾ lb) almond paste, cover the top and sides of the cake (see page 18).

Place a small basin or cup on the centre of the cake and mark a 10-cm (4-in) circle. Remove the basin and carefully cut through the depth of the cake; remove the inner small cake. Cover the inner ring and small cake side with almond paste. Leave both cakes to dry.

Coat the inner ring with icing. Coat the sides of both cakes with icing, smooth roughly with a palette knife and 'rib' the sides with a serrated icing comb (see page 19). Leave to dry for 24 hours. Flat ice the top of the ring cake and the small cake, using a palette knife or icing ruler to level the top. Leave to dry. Spread a thick layer of icing around the top and bottom rims of the ring cake and pull up into peaks using a palette knife or spoon. Finish the inner edge in the same way. Leave to dry for about 24 hours.

Attach the ribbon across the small cake. Using an icing bag fitted with an eight point star nozzle, pipe a shell border around the top and bottom edges of the small cake. Pipe one rosette on the top of the cake and position the candle. Leave to dry for about 24 hours. Arrange and fix holly leaves and berries to the lower edge. Attach holly leaves and berries to the inner edge of the ring cake and arrange and secure the run-out bells or Santa. Attach the ribbon around the side of the ring cake.

Simnel cake

You will need:
18-cm (7-in) round simnel cake (see page 123)
450 g (1 lb) almond paste
apricot glaze
egg white
white glacé icing using 100 g (4 oz) icing sugar etc.

Decoration
Easter chick (see page 47)

Divide the almond paste in half. Roll out the first half into a 18-cm (7-in) round. Brush the top of the cake with apricot glaze and place the almond paste on top. Mark into diamonds with a sharp knife.

Roll two-thirds of the remaining almond paste into eleven small balls. Roll out the remaining almond paste and cut out eleven flower shapes with a small fluted cutter. Roll the trimmings into the same number of tiny balls. Brush the almond paste on top of the cake with egg white and arrange the almond paste balls and flowers around the edge.

Brush the top of the cake with egg white and cook under a hot grill for 1–2 minutes, until golden brown. Leave to cool. Spoon a little icing in the centre of the cake and spread to a neat circle. Position the shell and chick on top of the icing.

Cakes for children's parties

Small children are always delighted with a novelty birthday cake, particularly if the cake depicts a favourite toy or story character. Not only is it a thrill for the children but if you are preparing a birthday spread, the cake immediately becomes the centre-piece of the party table. You can also include a selection of the smaller cakes featured in the Small cakes chapter earlier in the book — all children will love the Chocolate hedgehogs or Funny faces.

Baking shaped or larger cakes
If you want to make a shaped cake, such as a number or heart, you need to know how much mixture is required to fill the special tin. This is quite simply calculated using the guide below. This guide also applies to making a larger cake than suggested in the following novelty cake ideas.

For every *600 ml (1 pint)* of water the tin will hold, you will need mixture made with the ingredients listed below, so multiply up as required. Remember to fill the tin only as deep as you want the finished cake to be — not necessarily to the very top.

Victoria sandwich cake mixture
giving 600 ml (1 pint)

50 g (2 oz) butter or margarine
50 g (2 oz) caster sugar
1 egg
50 g (2 oz) self raising flour

Fruit cake mixture
giving 600 ml (1 pint)

175 g (6 oz) currants
50 g (2 oz) sultanas
50 g (2 oz) raisins, stoned
12 glacé cherries, halved
45 ml (3 tbsp) chopped mixed peel
100 g (3½ oz) plain flour
1·25 ml (¼ level tsp) mixed spice
75 g (3 oz) butter or margarine
75 g (3 oz) rich brown soft sugar
1½ eggs

Make either cake in the usual way (see pages 118 and 120). Bake the Victoria sandwich mixture in a moderate oven at 180°C (350°F) mark 4 and the fruit cake mixture in the oven at 150°C (300°F) mark 1–2. The time, of course, varies according to the shape and depth of the cake. Bake the *Victoria sandwich cake* until golden brown and well risen. Test to see if the cake is ready by gently pressing the surface of the cake with your finger. The cake should spring back and not leave an impression. The mixture should also have slightly shrunk away from the sides of the tin during baking. Once baked, leave the cake to cool for about 5 minutes before turning out of the tin on to a wire rack to cool completely. If you want to cook the cake a few days in advance of the party, wrap the completely cooled cake in cling film or foil and store in an airtight tin. When preparing a larger cake, you may prefer to cut the cake into three or four layers instead of two, so allow extra jam or make more butter cream for the extra filling.

Bake the *fruit cake* in the centre of the oven and test to see if cooked by piercing with a skewer — the skewer should come out clean. Leave the cake to cool completely in the tin before turning out.

When to decorate the cake
Cakes look fresher if iced on the day of the party, although you may prefer to do this the night or day before. Most of the decorated cakes featured in this chapter will store well in an airtight container, but not in the refrigerator as this will dry out the cake. *Glacé icing* will wrinkle if stored for more than 48 hours. The colouring in Smarties will 'bleed' into the icing so they should be added on the day. *Chocolate shapes* will absorb moisture from the icing and lose their crispness and become dull in appearance, so these should also be added on the day. It is still possible to decorate and assemble the rest of the cake in advance and just add the decorations later.

Cake boards
A silver cake board always enhances any iced cake but is not always vital. Several of the cakes featured in this chapter do need a base, so a large flat plate can be used instead, or a chopping board covered in foil is a good substitute. If you use a silver cake board, it can be used again providing the cake is carefully cut and the silver paper surface of the board is not damaged. After the party, wipe the board over carefully with a damp cloth then leave to dry completely before storing away. A damaged board can, of course, always be re-covered with a new piece of foil.

Animal maypole

Illustrated in colour facing page 96

You will need:
two 20·5-cm (8-in) round Victoria sandwich
  cakes
apricot jam
apricot butter cream using 325 g (12 oz) icing
  sugar etc.
28-cm (11-in) round cake board

Decoration
Smarties
chocolate finger biscuits
chocolate animal figures
coloured ribbon and drinking straw

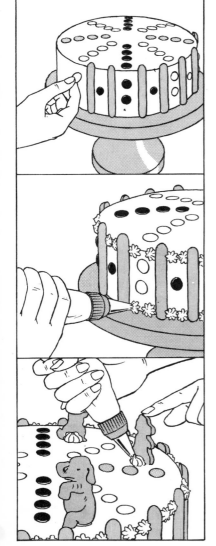

Spread the cakes with apricot jam and sandwich together. Place the cake on the cake board.

Spread two-thirds of the butter cream over the top and sides of the cake and smooth over with a palette knife.

Sort the Smarties according to colours. Place alternate rows of Smarties and chocolate finger biscuits around the side of the cake. Add rows of the same colours of Smarties to the top of the cake in a radial pattern.

Spoon the remaining butter cream into an icing bag fitted with an eight point star nozzle. Pipe two butter cream rosettes between each chocolate finger around the top and bottom edge of the cake.

Stand the chocolate animal figures around the top edge of the cake. Secure in position by piping a rosette behind each animal. Twist the coloured ribbons by pulling them from underneath the closed blades of a pair of scissors. Make a slit in the top of the straw and push the ribbons into it.

Pipe a rosette in the centre of the cake and insert the straw. Attach the ends of the ribbon to the back of the animals with a butter cream rosette.

Winter gingerbread house

Illustrated on the jacket

You will need:
20·5-cm (8-in) square ginger cake
white royal icing using 225 g (8 oz) icing
    sugar etc.
granulated sugar
28-cm (11-in) square cake board

Decoration
chocolate buttons
licorice allsorts

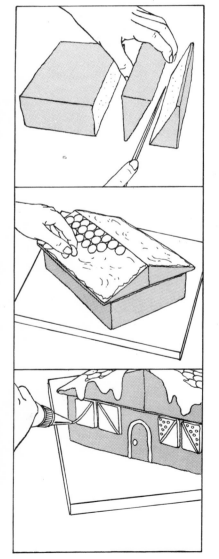

Measure 12·5 cm (5 in) along the cake and cut through for the base of the house. Cut the other piece of cake in half diagonally for the two halves of the roof. Place the base of the house on the cake board. Sandwich the two halves of the roof together with a little icing. Spread the top of the base with a little icing and place the sloping roof on top.

Spread the sloping surfaces of the roof with a thin layer of icing and arrange the chocolate buttons in a pattern for the tiles. Spoon a little icing on top of the roof for the snow, with a few icicles along the eaves. Position and fix the chimney.

Spoon some icing into an icing bag fitted with a plain nozzle (No. 2) and pipe in the doors at both ends of the house. Select square licorice allsorts for windows, attach to the house with icing and pipe in the curtains.
    Arrange the licorice allsorts around the base of the cake.
    Spread the remaining icing over the cake board around the house and swirl with the back of a spoon. Mark a pathway to the front and back doorway with a knife while the icing is still wet. Sprinkle the icing with the sugar. If liked, a simple snowman can be made from kneaded fondant icing using licorice allsorts for his hat and cloves for eyes, buttons and pipe.

Snakes and ladders cake

You will need:
1 quantity Victoria sandwich mixture baked in a
   20·5-cm (8-in) square cake tin
white glacé icing using 325 g (12 oz) icing
   sugar etc.
yellow food colouring
butter cream using 225 g (8 oz) icing sugar etc.
brown food colouring or cocoa powder
23-cm (9-in) square cake board

Decoration
100 g (4 oz) almond paste
green food colouring
Smarties

Spoon some icing into an icing bag fitted with a plain nozzle (No. 2). Pipe straight lines 5 cm (2 in) apart vertically and horizontally on top of the cake for the squares of the 'board' game.

Colour half the remaining icing yellow. Spoon yellow icing into alternate squares. Ease the icing into corners with a paint brush, skewer or tip of a knife. Spread the remaining icing on two opposite sides of the cake. Repeat, filling the empty squares with white icing and spread the remainder of the white icing on the other two sides and leave to set.

Place the cake on the cake board.

Colour a little of the butter cream chocolate and reserve. Colour the remainder yellow and spoon into an icing bag fitted with an eight point star nozzle. Pipe a shell border around the top and bottom of the cake. Spoon the chocolate butter cream into an icing bag fitted with a plain (No. 2) nozzle. Pipe in the four ladders.

Knead green food colouring into 75 g (3 oz) of the almond paste. Roll into snake shapes of varying thickness and length. Shape almond paste tongues for each snake and make indentations on the back of each snake with a knife. Pipe two dots with brown butter cream for eyes. Position on the cake.

Shape the remaining almond paste into a cube for the dice. Pipe dots on each face of the dice with chocolate butter cream. Place on the cake with Smarties for counters.

Treasure chest

Illustrated in colour facing page 112

You will need:

chocolate Victoria sandwich mixture baked in a
   900-g (2-lb) loaf tin (see page 104)
chocolate butter cream using 225 g (8 oz) icing
   sugar etc.
butter cream using 225 g (8 oz) icing sugar etc.
yellow food colouring
square cake board (optional)

Decoration
foil-covered chocolate coins
children's jewellery

Cut off the top third of the cake for the lid. Spread the sides of
the base of the cake with chocolate butter cream and smooth
over. Place the cake on the cake board.
   Spread the sides and top of the lid with chocolate butter
cream and smooth over.

Colour the plain butter cream a golden yellow and spoon into
an icing bag fitted with an eight point star nozzle. Pipe a shell
border at the base of the four sides of the chest. Pipe a
shell border down the four corners and around the top of the
chest then leave the icing until set. Pipe a shell border along
all the edges of the lid. Pipe two rows of shell border over the
top of the lid.

Spread some chocolate butter cream along the back edge of
the base of the chest to hold the lid in place. Arrange the
chocolate money and the jewellery over the top of the cake
and the cake board. Place the lid in an open position, supported by the money.

Yacht birthday cake

You will need:
1 quantity Victoria sandwich mixture baked in a
   20·5-cm (8-in) square cake tin
white glacé icing using 325 g (12 oz) icing
   sugar etc
blue food colouring
icing sugar
50 g (2 oz) almond paste
30·5-cm (12-in) square cake board

Decoration
5 white mint rings
white candles and holders

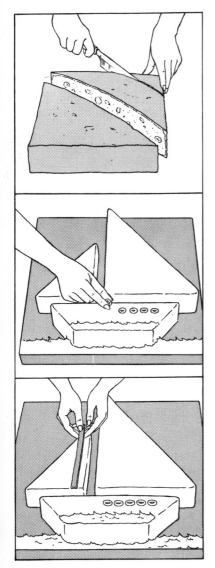

Cut the cake in half diagonally. Cut one half into two pieces to form the base of the yacht and the small sail.

Place the pieces of cake on a wire rack with a tray or plate underneath.

Colour half the glacé icing blue and leave the other half white. Coat the base of the boat in blue icing and the two sails in white icing. Leave until set.

Place the cakes in position on the cake board. Add enough icing sugar to the remaining white icing to make it stiff. Spread white icing along the bottom of the yacht base and on the board. Pull into well formed peaks with a knife or the back of a teaspoon to form waves. Place the mints in position for portholes.

Roll out half the almond paste on a surface dusted with sifted icing sugar. Cut into four thin strips, arrange on the small and large sails, secure with a little white icing. Divide the remaining almond paste into nine even-sized pieces. Roll and shape into flat balls, make an indentation in the centre of each. Place in position on the large sail, secure with a little white icing. Pipe 'Happy Birthday' in blue icing on the large sail. Place the candle holders and candles in the mint rings.

Medieval castle

Illustrated in colour facing page 97

You will need:

double quantity Victoria sandwich mixture baked
in two 18-cm (7-in) square cake tins
chocolate butter cream using 450 g (1 lb) icing
sugar etc.
green food colouring
50 g (2 oz) desiccated coconut
23-cm (11-in) square cake board

Decoration

24 2·5-cm (1-in) chocolate squares (see page 41)
3 chocolate finger biscuits
4 miniature paper flags and toy knights

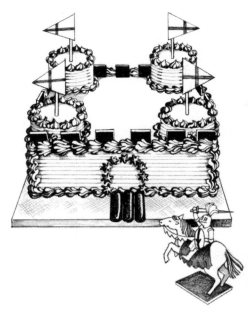

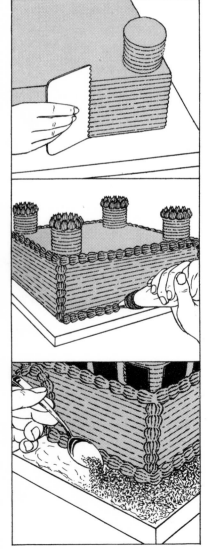

Cut eight 3·5 cm (1½ in) diameter rounds from one cake with a plain pastry cutter. Place the other cake on the cake board and spread the top and sides with the chocolate butter cream. Smooth the top of the cake with a palette knife. Using a serrated icing comb, mark the sides of the cake. For each tower, sandwich two rounds of cake together with butter cream. Stand one tower at each corner of the cake and spread the top and side with butter cream. Smooth over with a palette knife. Using the serrated icing comb, mark the side of each tower.

Spoon some butter cream into an icing bag fitted with an eight point star nozzle. Pipe a shell border around the top and base edges of the castle and down each corner. Pipe a star or shell edge around the top and base edges of each tower. Place the chocolate squares, evenly spaced, along the top edge of the castle. Pipe a doorway in the centre of two opposite sides.

Spread the cake board with butter cream. Stir a little green food colouring into the desiccated coconut and sprinkle liberally over the butter cream for grass. Cut the chocolate biscuits in half and place three halves in front of each door for the drawbridges. Place a flag in each tower. Place the toy knights in position.

Butterfly cake

Illustrated in colour facing page 96

You will need:
1 quantity Victoria sandwich mixture baked in a
    20.5-cm (8-in) square cake tin
butter cream using 225 g (8 oz) icing sugar etc.
white glacé icing using 325 g (12 oz) icing
    sugar etc.
pink food colouring
30·5-cm (12-in) square cake board

Decoration
chocolate covered fudge bar
silver balls
thin wire

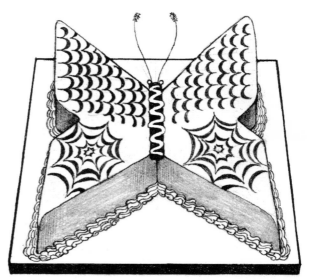

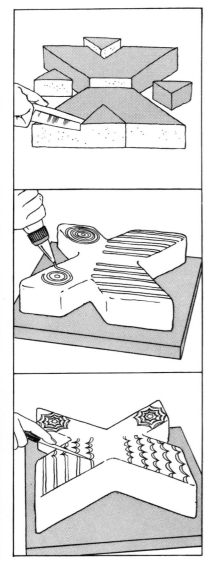

Cut the cake in half diagonally. Cut off the two corners opposite the long straight side. Cut a 'V' shaped piece from each half to form the wings. (Use the trimmings for a trifle.)

Spread a little butter cream on the cut corner of each half and join together to form a butterfly shape.

Place the butterfly on a wire rack with a plate underneath. Colour 60 ml (4 tbsp) white glacé icing pink and spoon into a greaseproof icing bag without a nozzle. Use half the remaining glacé icing to coat the top and sides of the cake. Place the butterfly on the cake board. Snip the end from the icing bag and pipe parallel straight lines on the top two butterfly wings and circles on the other two.

Work quickly before the icing has time to set. First draw a skewer or pointed knife across the piped lines in one direction only to make the feather pattern. Then draw the skewer or knife from the centre of the circles to the outside edge. Leave to set.

Pipe a pink zig-zag line down the fudge bar. Pipe in two eyes at one end and top with silver balls. Place in position for the body and insert the wire for the antennae.

Colour the butter cream pink, place in an icing bag fitted with an eight point star nozzle. Pipe a shell border around the base of the butterfly.

Humpty Dumpty

Illustrated in colour opposite

You will need:

1 quantity Victoria sandwich mixture baked in a
  900-g (2-lb) loaf tin for about 45 minutes at
  190°C (375°F) mark 5
apricot jam
cocoa powder
kneaded fondant icing using 450 g (1 lb) icing
  sugar etc.
pink, yellow and green food colourings
rectangular or square cake board (optional)

Cut the cake in half horizontally, spread the cut surfaces with jam and sandwich together. Knead enough cocoa powder into two-thirds of the fondant icing to colour it pale brown. Roll out thinly to a rectangle on a surface lightly dusted with sifted icing sugar. Cut a rectangle the same size as the top of the cake, two strips the depth of the cake for the sides and two rectangles for the ends of the cake. Spread the sides with jam and place the chocolate fondant in position. Place the cake on a cake board or flat plate. Use a pointed knife to mark the brick pattern on the wall.

Colour half the remaining fondant a pale apricot, using the pink and yellow colouring, and mould into Humpty Dumpty's head, legs, arms and hands. Use extra icing sugar when rolling out to dust the board and prevent the icing from becoming too soft. Use a little fondant to make Humpty a hat and a pair of boots. Assemble by pushing the pieces gently but firmly together. Paint in his facial features with food colouring.

Divide the remaining white fondant icing into three pieces; colour one pink, one green and one yellow. Cut out and mould pink and yellow flowers, and green leaves and stalks. Place Humpty in position on the cake and push down gently until sitting securely on the wall. Decorate the wall with flowers and leaves and hold in place with a little jam.

Humpty Dumpty (*page 112*), Treasure chest (*page 108*),
Balloon cake (*page 116*)

Tate and Lyle Sugars. Nothing else can hold a candle to them!

Tate and Lyle make a whole range of Special Sugars. As well as Icing, there's Caster, London Demerara, Preserving and Brown Soft Sugars.

Each one's specially created for a different job. All of them will give your cooking and baking an extra special quality.

Number birthday cake

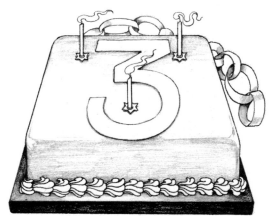

You will need:
1 quantity Victoria sandwich mixture baked in an
   18-cm (7-in) square cake tin
raspberry jam
glacé icing using 700 g (1½ lb) icing sugar etc.
pink or blue food colouring
butter cream using 225 g (8 oz) icing sugar etc.
23-cm (9-in) square cake board (optional)

Decoration
pink or blue candles
pink or blue candle holders

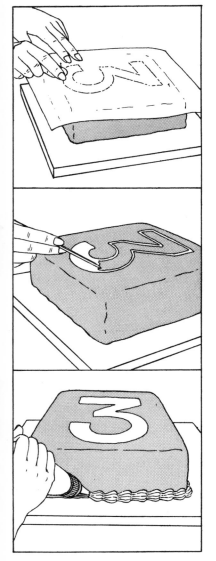

Cut the cake in half horizontally, spread the cut surfaces with jam and sandwich together. Reserve one-third of the glacé icing and colour the remaining icing pink or blue. Place the cake on a wire rack with a plate underneath and pour the coloured icing over the cake. Spread to cover the top and sides completely. Leave until set. Place the cake on the cake board. Draw the appropriate number on a square of grease-proof paper, the same size as the top of the cake. Place this pattern on the top of the cake and carefully prick out the outline of the number with a pin, without applying any pressure to the surface of the cake.

Spoon some of the reserved white glacé icing into a grease-proof icing bag fitted with a plain nozzle (No. 2). Pipe a line around the outline of the number following the pin pricks. Using a teaspoon, carefully spoon the white icing between the piped lines and ease to the edges with the point of a skewer.

Colour the butter cream a darker pink or blue than the glacé icing and spoon into an icing bag fitted with an eight point star nozzle. Pipe a shell border around the bottom edge of the cake. Place the candles and candle holders in position.

Note Although tins in the shape of numbers are available and can sometimes be hired, unless they can be used more than once the price of the tin makes the cake rather expensive. Therefore, this run-out is a useful alternative.

Chocolate goods train

You will need:
1 quantity Victoria sandwich
    mixture baked in an 18-cm
    (7-in) square cake tin
1 chocolate Swiss roll
chocolate butter cream using
    450 g (1 lb) icing sugar etc.

Decoration
small ginger biscuits
chocolate finger biscuits
Smarties
licorice allsorts

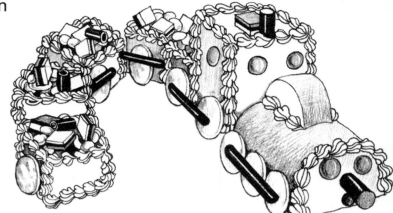

Cut the square cake in half and one half into four equal pieces. Cut one piece from the remaining cake the same size as the other four. Cut a slice from one end of the Swiss roll and reserve.

Place the Swiss roll in position for the engine and stand the large piece of cake upright behind the Swiss roll for the cab. Place one smaller piece of cake behind for the fender and the remaining four pieces spaced behind for trucks.

Spread the train and trucks with half the butter cream. Spread a little icing on the back of each ginger biscuit and gently push into the sides of the train and each truck for wheels.

Spread a little butter cream on the back of each chocolate finger biscuit and push gently into position on top of the ginger biscuits. Spoon the remaining butter cream into an icing bag fitted with an eight point star nozzle. Cut the slice of Swiss roll in half and place one piece in position on the train.

Pipe a shell border on the edges of the train and the trucks. Place the Smarties in place for the 'face' and windows on the train and a licorice allsort for the nose and chimney. Fill the fender and trucks with licorice allsorts.

Daisy cake

Illustrated in colour facing page 96

You will need:
two 20·5-cm (8-in) round Victoria sandwich cakes
raspberry jam
glacé icing using 325 g (12 oz) icing sugar etc.
pink food colouring
kneaded fondant icing using 225 g (8 oz) icing
    sugar etc.
butter cream using 225 g (8 oz) icing sugar etc.
28-cm (11-in) round cake board (optional)

Decoration
pink candle holders
white or pink candles

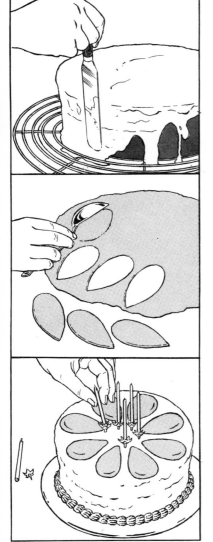

Sandwich the cakes together with raspberry jam. Place on a wire rack with a tray or large plate underneath to catch any surplus icing. Colour the glacé icing pink and pour over the cake. Spread over the top and side, making sure the cake is completely covered. Leave to set and then place on the cake board.

Draw a large petal shape on a piece of greaseproof paper, using a dessert spoon as a guide. Cut out and use as a pattern. Knead the fondant icing until pliable. Roll out to 0·5 cm ($\frac{1}{4}$ in) thick on a surface dusted with sifted icing sugar.

    Place the greaseproof pattern on the fondant icing and cut out nine or ten large petals. Mould the outside edges of the petals upwards. Place the petals in a circle around the top of the cake, leaving a space in the centre for the candles.

Colour the butter cream a darker pink than the glacé icing. Spoon into an icing bag fitted with an eight point star nozzle. Pipe a shell border around the base of the cake. Place the candles in a neat ring in the centre of the cake.

Balloon cake

Illustrated in colour facing page 112

You will need:

two 20·5-cm (8-in) round Victoria sandwich cakes
chocolate butter cream using 325 g (12 oz) icing
     sugar etc.
23-cm (9-in) round cake board

Decoration
4 drinking straws
coloured balloon
coloured ribbon
almond paste boy and girl (see page 47)
selection of small sweets

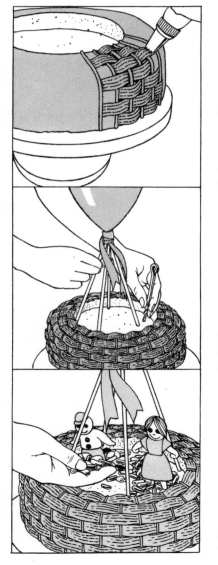

Cut a 15-cm (6-in) diameter hollow in one cake and use the centre in another recipe. Sandwich the cakes together with a little butter cream. Place on the cake board.

Divide the remaining icing, place half in an icing bag fitted with a plain nozzle (No. 2) and half in a bag fitted with a basket nozzle. Pipe a vertical line down the side of the cake using the plain nozzle. Pipe short horizontal lines with the basket nozzle, spaced evenly over the vertical line. Continue around the side of the cake to complete the basket (see page 29).

Make four holes inside the basket with a skewer. Place the four straws in the holes at the edge of the cake. Attach the balloon to the straws with a little sticky tape. Tie the piece of ribbon over the tape.

Place the almond paste figures in position in the basket, securing with a little butter cream if necessary. Scatter the sweets around them, making sure the sponge is covered.

Windmill

You will need:

1 quantity Victoria sandwich mixture baked in a
   23-cm (9-in) square cake tin
butter cream using 325 g (12 oz) icing sugar etc.
orange, green and pink food colouring
desiccated coconut
20·5-cm (8-in) square cake board

Decoration
two 2·5-cm (1-in) chocolate squares (see page 41)
2 chocolate door shapes
4 chocolate triangles, 10 cm (4 in) long (see page 41)
50 g (2 oz) almond paste
almond paste boy and girl (see page 47)

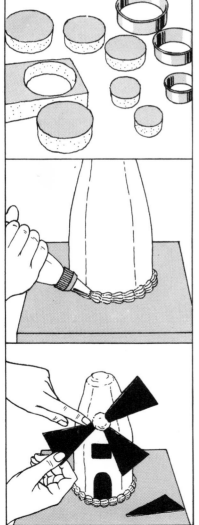

Cut two 10-cm (4-in), two 7·5-cm (3-in) and two 5-cm (2-in) diameter rounds from the sandwich cake. Colour the butter cream a pale orange. Spread the top of each round with a little butter cream. Pile up the rounds with the smallest ones at the top. Place the cake on the board.

Spread the windmill with butter cream and smooth over with a palette knife. Spoon some of the butter cream into a piping bag fitted with an eight point star nozzle. Pipe a shell border around the base of the cake. Gently press the chocolate square windows and the chocolate doors in place. Spread the board lightly with butter cream. Stir a little green food colouring into the coconut and spoon on to the butter cream for grass.

Pipe a large rosette near the top of the windmill and position the four chocolate triangles for the sails. Divide the almond paste into two pieces and knead pink food colouring into one and green food colouring into the other. Roll out on a surface dusted with sifted icing sugar. Cut the pink almond paste into flower shapes and the green into stalks and leaves. Place in position around the base of the windmill. Place the almond paste figures on the board.

Cake recipes

We have included a selection of cake recipes so you can choose the right type of cake for your particular requirements.

The Rich fruit cake recipe is ideal for all the 'Special occasion' cakes; look at the useful chart opposite to calculate the amount of cake mixture required to fill the tin or tins you are using. In case the family prefer a lighter fruit cake, we have included a recipe for one. It produces a less firm cake which can also be made in advance and stored.

There are a selection of sponge and sandwich cake recipes. The popular Victoria sandwich will store most successfully — for about 3–4 days in an airtight tin. The Genoese is a lighter, more airy sponge that will only keep for 1–2 days. The whisked sponge recipe is also used to make a Swiss roll; this sponge is very light and airy, and because it is fatless it should be eaten on the day it is made. Use any of these sponge cake recipes for the cakes in Chapter 4 or for the Children's party cakes, using the variations to flavour the cakes if liked.

A ginger cake recipe has been included for the Winter gingerbread house in Chapter 6, and the Simnel cake recipe has been beautifully decorated on page 103.

Special occasion cakes

The following method applies to the cakes in the chart on the opposite page

Line the cake tin, or tins, of your choice, using two thicknesses of greaseproof paper. Tie a double band of brown paper round the outside. Clean the fruit if necessary. Mix the prepared currants, sultanas, raisins, cherries, peel, almonds and lemon rind together. Sift the flour and the spices. Cream the butter and sugar until pale and fluffy. Add the beaten eggs, a little at a time, beating well after each addition. Fold in half the flour, using a metal spoon, then fold in the rest and add the brandy. Lastly fold in the fruit. Spoon into the cake tin or tins. Spread the mixture evenly, making sure there are no air pockets, and make a dip in the centre. Stand the tin or tins on a layer of newspaper or brown paper in the oven and bake at 150°C (300°F) mark 1–2 for the time indicated in the chart opposite. With the larger sizes, 25 cm (10 in) and upwards, it is advisable to reduce the oven heat to 130°C (250°F) mark ½ after two-thirds of the cooking time. To avoid over-browning the top, cover it with several thicknesses of greaseproof paper after 1½ hours. When the cake is cooked, leave to cool in the tin then turn out on to a wire rack. Prick the cake top all over with a fine skewer and slowly pour 30–45 ml (2–3 tbsp) brandy over it before storing.

To store, wrap the cake in several layers of greaseproof paper and place in an airtight tin. If a large enough storage tin is not available, cover the wrapped cake entirely in foil.

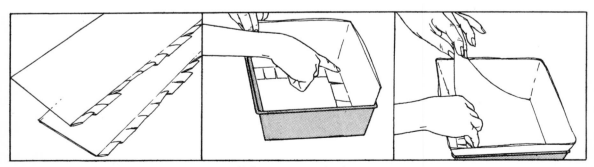

Lining a square cake tin

Quantities and sizes for special occasion cakes

If you want to make a formal cake for a birthday, wedding or anniversary, the following chart will show you the amount of ingredients required to fill the chosen cake tin or tins, whether round or square.

	15 cm (6 in) square / 18 cm (7 in) round	18 cm (7 in) square / 20.5 cm (8 in) round	20.5 cm (8 in) square / 23 cm (9 in) round	23 cm (9 in) square / 25.5 cm (10 in) round	25.5 cm (10 in) square / 28 cm (11 in) round	28 cm (11 in) square / 30.5 cm (12 in) round	30.5 cm (12 in) square
Currants	225 g (8 oz)	450 g (1 lb)	625 g (1 lb 6 oz)	775 g (1 lb 12 oz)	1.1 kg (2 lb 8 oz)	1.5 kg (3 lb 2 oz)	1.7 kg (3 lb 12 oz)
Sultanas	100 g (3½ oz)	200 g (7 oz)	225 g (8 oz)	375 g (13 oz)	400 g (14 oz)	525 g (1 lb 3 oz)	625 g (1 lb 6 oz)
Raisins	100 g (3½ oz)	200 g (7 oz)	225 g (8 oz)	375 g (13 oz)	400 g (14 oz)	525 g (1 lb 3 oz)	625 g (1 lb 6 oz)
Glacé cherries	50 g (2 oz)	150 g (5 oz)	175 g (6 oz)	250 g (9 oz)	275 g (10 oz)	350 g (12 oz)	425 g (15 oz)
Mixed peel	25 g (1 oz)	75 g (3 oz)	100 g (4 oz)	150 g (5 oz)	200 g (7 oz)	250 g (9 oz)	275 g (10 oz)
Almonds	25 g (1 oz)	75 g (3 oz)	100 g (4 oz)	150 g (5 oz)	200 g (7 oz)	250 g (9 oz)	275 g (10 oz)
Lemon rind	a little	a little	¼ lemon	¼ lemon	½ lemon	½ lemon	1 lemon
Plain flour	175 g (6 oz)	350 g (12 oz)	400 g (14 oz)	600 g (1 lb 5 oz)	700 g (1 lb 8 oz)	825 g (1 lb 13 oz)	1 kg (2 lb 6 oz)
Mixed spice	1.25 ml (¼ level tsp)	2.5 ml (½ level tsp)	5 ml (1 level tsp)	5 ml (1 level tsp)	10 ml (2 level tsp)	12.5 ml (2½ level tsp)	12.5 ml (2½ level tsp)
Cinnamon	1.25 ml (¼ level tsp)	2.5 ml (½ level tsp)	5 ml (1 level tsp)	5 ml (1 level tsp)	10 ml (2 level tsp)	12.5 ml (2½ level tsp)	12.5 ml (2½ level tsp)
Butter	150 g (5 oz)	275 g (10 oz)	350 g (12 oz)	500 g (1 lb 2 oz)	600 g (1 lb 5 oz)	800 g (1 lb 12 oz)	950 g (2 lb 2 oz)
Sugar	150 g (5 oz)	275 g (10 oz)	350 g (12 oz)	500 g (1 lb 2 oz)	600 g (1 lb 5 oz)	800 g (1 lb 12 oz)	950 g (2 lb 2 oz)
Large eggs, beaten	2½	5	6	9	11	14	17
Brandy	15 ml (1 tbsp)	15–30 ml (1–2 tbsp)	30 ml (2 tbsp)	30–45 ml (2–3 tbsp)	45 ml (3 tbsp)	60 ml (4 tbsp)	90 ml (6 tbsp)
Time (approx)	2½–3 hours	3½ hours	4 hours	6 hours	7 hours	8 hours	8½ hours
Weight when cooked	1.1 kg (2½ lb)	2.2 kg (4¾ lb)	2.7 kg (6 lb)	4 kg (9 lb)	5.2 kg (11½ lb)	6.7 kg (14¾ lb)	7.7 kg (17 lb)

Note For icing and almond paste quantities see page 71.

Lining a round cake tin

Light fruit cake

175 g (6 oz) glacé cherries, halved
175 g (6 oz) currants
175 g (6 oz) sultanas
100 g (4 oz) glacé pineapple
225 g (8 oz) butter or margarine
225 g (8 oz) caster sugar
50 g (2 oz) ground almonds
4 eggs, beaten
225 g (8 oz) self raising flour
100 g (4 oz) mixed cut peel, chopped
grated rind and juice of 1 lemon
45 ml (3 tbsp) brandy

This light fruit cake is best stored for 1–2 weeks before eating.

Line a 23-cm (9-in) round or 20·5-cm (8-in) square cake tin, using a double thickness of greaseproof paper. If the cherries are very syrupy, wash them and dry well. Clean the currants and sultanas if necessary. Cut the glacé pineapple into small cubes. Cream the butter and sugar until pale and fluffy and stir in the ground almonds. Add the beaten egg, a little at a time, beating well after each addition. Add 45 ml (3 level tbsp) of the flour to the fruits and peel, mixing well. Fold these ingredients, alternately with the rest of the flour, the grated lemon rind and lemon juice into the creamed mixture. Lastly, stir in the brandy. Put the mixture into the tin and bake in the oven at 170°C (325°F) mark 3 for about 2½ hours, or until risen and just firm to the touch. Cool and store as for Rich fruit cake.

Note If a firmer cake is preferred, use 100 g (4 oz) self raising flour and 125 g (4 oz) plain flour.

Victoria sandwich cake

175 g (6 oz) butter or margarine
175 g (6 oz) caster sugar
3 eggs, beaten
175 g (6 oz) self raising flour
30 ml (2 tbsp) jam
caster sugar to dredge

Grease two 20-cm (8-in) straight-sided sandwich tins and line the base of each with a round of greased greaseproof paper. Cream the butter or margarine and sugar until pale and fluffy. Add the beaten egg a little at a time, beating well after each addition. Fold in half the flour, using a metal spoon, then fold in the rest. Place half the mixture in each tin and level it with a knife. Bake the cakes on separate shelves of the oven at 190°C (375°F) mark 5 for about 20—25 minutes, or until they are well risen, golden, firm to the touch and beginning to shrink away from the sides of the tins. Turn out and cool on a wire rack.

VARIATIONS

Chocolate

Replace 45 ml (3 level tbsp) flour with 45 ml (3 level tbsp) cocoa powder. Sandwich together with vanilla or chocolate butter cream. For a moister cake, blend the cocoa with water to give a thick paste. Beat into the creamed ingredients.

Orange or lemon

Add the finely grated rind of 1 orange or lemon to the mixture. Sandwich the cakes together with orange or lemon curd or orange or lemon butter cream. Use some of the juice from the fruit to make glacé icing.

Coffee

Add 10 ml (2 level tsp) instant coffee powder dissolved in a little warm water to the creamed mixture with the egg. Or use 10 ml (2 tsp) coffee essence.

Lining a sandwich cake tin

One stage sandwich cake

This is a very quick method to make a sandwich cake without creaming the fat first — but you must use soft tub margarine.

175 g (6 oz) self raising flour
7·5 ml (1½ level tsp) baking powder
175 g (6 oz) soft tub margarine
175 g (6 oz) caster sugar
3 eggs

Grease two 20·5-cm (8-in) sandwich tins and line each base with a round of greased greaseproof paper. Sift the flour and baking powder into a large bowl. Add the other ingredients, mix well, then beat for about 2 minutes. Divide the mixture evenly between the tins. Bake in the oven at 170°C (325°F) mark 3 for 25—35 minutes until golden brown and well risen. Turn out and cool on a wire rack.

VARIATIONS

Orange

Add the grated rind and juice of 1 orange.

Mocha

Sift 30 ml (2 level tbsp) cocoa powder and 15 ml (1 level tbsp) instant coffee powder with 150 g (5-oz) flour and the baking powder.

Chocolate

Sift 45 ml (3 level tbsp) cocoa powder with 150 g (5 oz) flour and the baking powder.

Genoese sponge

40 g (1½ oz) butter
75 g (2½ oz) plain flour
15 ml (1 level tbsp) cornflour
3 large eggs
75 g (3 oz) caster sugar

Grease and line two 20-cm (8-in) straight-sided sandwich tins. Heat the butter gently until melted, remove from the heat and let it stand for a few minutes, for the salt and sediment to settle.

Sift the flour and cornflour. Place the eggs and sugar in a large bowl, stand this over a saucepan of hot water and whisk until light and creamy — the mixture should be stiff enough to retain the impression of the whisk for a few seconds. Remove from the heat and whisk until cool. Re-sift the flour and cornflour and carefully fold in half with a metal spoon. Make sure the butter is cooled until it *just* flows and, taking care not to let the salt and sediment run in, pour the butter a little at a time round the edge of the mixture. Then fold in alternately with the rest of the flour. Fold very lightly or the melted butter will sink to the bottom and make a heavy cake. Pour the mixture into the tins and bake in the oven at 190°C (375°F) mark 5 for about 20–25 minutes until golden brown and firm to the touch. Turn out and cool on a wire rack.

Note If you are using an electric mixer, no heat is required during whisking.

Whisked sponge

3 eggs
100 g (4 oz) caster sugar
75 g (3 oz) plain flour

Grease two 20-cm (8-in) straight-sided sandwich tins and dust with a mixture of flour and caster sugar. Put the eggs and sugar in a large deep bowl, stand this over a pan of hot water and whisk until light and creamy – the mixture should be stiff enough to retain the impression of the whisk for a few seconds. Remove from the heat and whisk until cold. Sift half the flour over the mixture and fold in very lightly, using a metal spoon. Add the remaining flour in the same way. Pour the mixture into the tins, tilting backwards and forwards until it is spread evenly and bake in the oven at 190°C (375°F) mark 5 for 20–25 minutes. Turn out to cool on a wire rack.

Note If you are using an electric mixer, no heat is required during whisking.

VARIATION

Chocolate whisked sponge
Replace 15 ml (1 level tbsp) of the flour with 15 ml (1 level tbsp) sieved cocoa powder.

Swiss roll

3 eggs
100 g (4 oz) caster sugar
100 g (4 oz) plain flour
15 ml (1 tbsp) hot water
caster sugar to dredge
warm jam

Line a Swiss roll tin 33·6 × 22·5 cm (13 × 9 in). Place the eggs and sugar in a large bowl, stand it over a pan of hot water and whisk until light and creamy – the mixture should be stiff enough to retain the impression of the whisk for a few seconds. Remove the bowl from the heat and whisk until cool. Sift half the flour over the mixture and fold in very lightly, using a metal spoon. Add the remaining flour in the same way and lightly stir in the hot water. Pour the mixture into the prepared tin, tilt the tin backwards and forwards allowing the mixture to run over the whole surface. Bake in the oven at 220°C (425°F) mark 7 for 7–9 minutes until golden brown, well risen and spongy. Meanwhile, have ready a sheet of greaseproof paper liberally sprinkled with caster sugar. To help make the sponge pliable you can place the paper over a tea towel lightly wrung out in hot water.

Turn the cake quickly out on to the paper, trim off the crusty edges with a sharp knife and spread the surface with warmed jam. Roll up with the aid of the paper, making the first turn firmly so that the whole cake will roll evenly and have a good shape when finished,

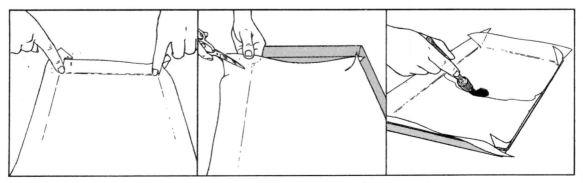

Lining a Swiss roll tin

but roll more lightly after this turn. Dredge the cake with sugar and cool on a wire rack.

Note If you are using an electric mixer no heat is required during whisking.

VARIATION

Chocolate Swiss roll

Replace 15 ml (1 level tbsp) flour by 15 ml (1 level tbsp) cocoa powder. If you are using a butter cream filling, turn out the cooked sponge and trim as above, but do not spread with the filling immediately. Cover the sponge with a sheet of greaseproof paper and roll it up loosely. When the cake is cold, unroll, remove paper, spread with cream or butter cream and re-roll.

Simnel cake

175 g (6 oz) almond paste
350 g (12 oz) currants
100 g (4 oz) sultanas
75 g (3 oz) mixed cut peel, chopped
225 g (8 oz) plain flour
pinch salt
5 ml (1 level tsp) ground cinnamon
5 ml (1 level tsp) ground nutmeg
175 g (6 oz) butter or margarine
175 g (6 oz) caster sugar
3 eggs, beaten

Line an 18-cm (7-in) round cake tin. Roll the almond paste into a round slightly smaller than the size of the cake tin. Clean the fruit if necessary. Mix the prepared currants, sultanas and peel. Sift the flour, salt and spices. Cream the butter and sugar until pale and fluffy. Add the beaten eggs, a little at a time, beating well after each addition. Fold in half the flour, using a metal spoon, then fold in the rest and lastly fold in the fruit. Spoon half the mixture into the prepared tin, smooth over the top and cover with almond paste. Cover with remaining mixture. Bake in the oven at 170°C (325°F) mark 3 for about 1 hour, then reduce to 150°C (300°F) mark 2 for 3 hours until the cake is golden brown and firm to the touch. Cool in the tin. Turn out and remove the greaseproof paper. See page 103 for decorating the cake.

Ginger cake

175 g (6 oz) butter or margarine
100 g (4 oz) caster sugar
60 ml (4 tbsp) golden syrup
4 eggs, beaten
450 g (1 lb) self raising flour
25 ml (1½ level tbsp) ground ginger

Grease and line a 23-cm (9-in) round or a 20·5-cm (8-in) square cake tin. Cream the butter or margarine, sugar and syrup together until pale and fluffy. Add the egg a little at a time, beating well after each addition. Fold in half the sifted flour and ginger using a metal spoon, then fold in the remaining flour. Spoon into the tin and bake in the oven at 170°C (325°F) mark 3 for about 1½ hours until golden and firm to the touch. Turn out and cool on a wire rack.

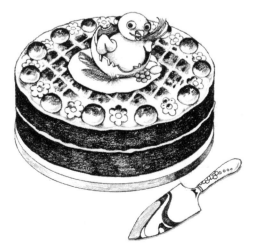

Addresses

Equipment

Nutbrown
Wilkinson Sword Ltd
Sword House
Totteridge Road
High Wycombe
Buckinghamshire
HP13 6EJ.
Tel: High Wycombe 33300

Metal Box Ltd
Queen's House
Forbury Road
Reading
Berkshire
RH1 3JH.
Tel: Reading 581177

G. T. Culpitt and Son Ltd
PO Box 77
Culpitt House
74–78 Town Centre
Hatfield
Hertfordshire
AL10 0AW.
Tel: Hatfield 65516

Mary Ford Cake Artistry Centre
28–30 Southbourne Grove
Bournemouth
Dorset
BH6 3RA.
Tel: Bournemouth 422653

Baker Smith (Cake Decorators Ltd)
65 The Street
Tongham
Farnham Surrey GU10 1DD.
Tel: Runfold 2984

Decorations

Flowers, silver leaves, candles etc.

Baker Smith (Cake Decorators Ltd)
(see under Equipment)

G. T. Culpitt and Son Ltd
(see under Equipment)

Mary Ford Cake Artistry Centre
(see under Equipment)

Anniversary House
23–25 Abbot Road
Winton
Bournemouth
Dorset
BH9 1EY.
Tel: Bournemouth 512221

Boards, pillars etc.

Baker Smith (Cake Decorators Ltd)
(see under Equipment)

G. T. Culpitt and Son Ltd
(see under Equipment)

Mary Ford Cake Artistry Centre
(see under Equipment)

For further information on modelling almond paste see
Modelling with Marzipan by James Winterflood. Apply direct
to the publishers: John F. Renshaw & Co Ltd, Locks Lane,
Mitcham, Surrey. Tel: 01–648 3005.

Index